Mrs Gregory Smith

Notes of travel in Mexico and California

Mrs Gregory Smith

Notes of travel in Mexico and California

ISBN/EAN: 9783337208158

Printed in Europe, USA, Canada, Australia, Japan

Cover: Foto ©Andreas Hilbeck / pixelio.de

More available books at **www.hansebooks.com**

Notes of Travel

IN

Mexico and California.

BY MRS. J. GREGORY SMITH,
AUTHOR OF
"Seola," "Atla," Etc.

Musa. "Was there more of pleasure or peril in thy journeyings?
Varus. " Listen to my story and thou shalt learn."

St. Albans, Vermont:
Printed at the Messenger and Advertiser Office.
1886.

Preface.

THE following NOTES OF TRAVEL, made during a journey to the Pacific Coast, were designed for private use only, but by request of many friends were subsequently arranged in form of letters to the *St. Albans Messenger*. The demand for the series was so much greater than had been anticipated, we were unable to meet the call for entire setts, and have therefore been induced to republish these very interesting letters in book-form.

EDITOR ST. ALBANS MESSENGER.

Table of Contents.

CHAPTER.		PAGE.
I.	On the Way to Mexico,	5
II.	In Ancient Aztlan,	13
III.	On the Mexican Central Railroad,	21
IV.	The City of Mexico	30
V.	The Halls of Montezuma,	42
VI.	Vera Cruz,	52
VII.	Farewell to Mexico,	60
VIII.	Los Angeles,	71
IX.	Monterey,	78
X.	Monterey,	87
XI.	San Francisco,	96
XII.	The Return,	103
XIII.	Salt Lake City and the Mormons,	109
XIV.	Homeward Bound,	120

Chapter One.

ON THE WAY TO MEXICO.

WE PROPOSE A JOURNEY—THE DECISION—LA JUNTA—RATON PASS—WONDERS OF RAILROAD ENGINEERING—A CANYON—THE RIO GRANDE—THE OLD SANTA FE TRAIL—A VALLEY OF DEATH—EL PASO—IN MEXICO—MISSION WINE.

WHEN shall we take our vacation? And where shall we go? The first query is easily answered—February and March are the most ungenial months of the year in this northern climate; then wind and storm hold revel, our heads are enveloped in gray mist, our footsteps impeded by drifting snow, chill blasts pierce the garments we have stolen from seal and bear, human strength falters in the prolonged struggle with cold and darkness.

Compel those dreary days to "straggle from the files of winter," supply their place with balmy breezes and blossoms of south-land.

Where shall we go? To the south of Europe, to Bermuda or Florida?

Tempt not the rough Atlantic in its season of storms; venture not upon the coral mushroom called Bermuda till the tempest and earthquake cycle is accomplished; seek not thy respite in the crowded hotels and malarious swamps of Florida.

But far away on the Pacific slope are lands to us unknown and fair. There will our fight with savage nature cease, and no longer stumbling on, manacled by muffs, mittens and arctics, we shall, like the Athenians of old, "delicately march in pelucid air." We must cross deserts and scale mountains till we reach the Eden of the West and tread the Halls of Montezuma.

Enough, enough! To the Halls of Montezuma we will go!

The decision was final, necessary preparations were made, the car "Bellevue" was put in order, accounts were settled, for who knew if we should ever return, and on February 16th we sailed out of St. Albans harbor, followed by the kind wishes of numerous friends who had gathered to witness our departure.

At Chicago we were delayed two days by business, and on February 20th we left that city and crossed the Mississippi river at Rock Island in the night, passed through a corner of Iowa, Missouri and the state of Kansas, emerging into mountainous Colorado February 22, reaching La Junta at ten o'clock a. m., a wild place marked by low wooden and adobe buildings and distant snow-capped mountains. While the other passengers breakfasted we took a brisk walk in the delicious air. Among the motley groups upon the platform was one that suggested sad and painful thought: a sheriff and two manacled convicts, one a brutal, dark-faced half-breed, the other a white man, with a repulsive but weaker expression—a tool rather than a master. To a query the sheriff replied: "These men have just finished a term in an eastern prison and are going to Arizona to be tried for another offense.

After leaving La Junta we entered the Raton Mountains and made the terrible Raton Pass, at an altitude of 7,700 feet above the sea and in sight of the majestic snow-crowned Spanish Mountains and Pike's Peak. These mountains were in view for hours, and although eighty miles away they appeared no more than fifteen miles distant. The railroad through these heights is a miracle of engineering; in one place the solid rock is tunnelled for a long distance, and in another there is a horseshoe curve up a grade of eighty-five feet to the mile, so sharp that the laboring, puffing giant in front of the train, and the panting, coughing pusher in the rear can be seen by the amazed occupants of the cars at the same instant. The frowning rocks overhead, the awful chasms beneath, the railroad train threading its way along the dizzy steeps, the wild loneliness of earth and the serenity of the cloudless sky form a picture never to be forgotten. A sense of imminent danger adds to the excitement of the scene. The tremendous pressure against the rails in this sharp curve causes the timbers of the car and wheels to grind and creak—even jump under the terrible strain.

We passed the deepest canyon in the night; a waning, melancholy moon increased the gloom of the dark shadows, as upward and onward the panting engine toiled, so slowly that it seemed about to give out through exhaustion. The curse of sin still hangs over mankind, toilers of the mountains, toilers of the sea. How insignificant, how helpless were we in this invasion of nature's fastness, where retreat or even faltering would be fatal. One could but exclaim with Dante, in the Inferno: "All hope abandon, ye who enter here."

We passed the dangerous point in safety and descended to the valley of the Rio Grande, a wide, straggling, irresponsible stream, changing one channel for another upon the slightest provocation; leaving, in its erratic course, dreary mudbanks, great drifts of stone and gravel, dangerous quicksands and shapeless pools; a river grand is nothing but treachery and irresponsibility. It led us into a broad and desolate plain, without tree or shrub, without rill or spring for seventy-two miles. This gloomy land, flanked on every side by dark, barren mountains, strange in shape and deceptive in distance, is part of the old Santa Fe Trail, and is aptly called The Valley of Death. Huge heaps of sand, driven by the blasts of a thousand years, beds of black lava, belched from the craters of long-forgotten volcanoes, and misshapened mounds of clay, mark this plateau as the battlefield of the enraged elements. No doubt it was once the domain of old ocean, but the internal fires of earth, roused by some tremendous cosmic influence, lifted the floor of waters with Titanic strength, heaving it upward till the helpless floods left their ancient basin and rushed away to seek another resting place. The imprisoned fires then burst through the rocky crust of earth and made an outlet for their fury through raging volcanoes. These poured forth flames, lava, ashes and noxious gases, till the land was made desolate past redemption. Not even a crow flaps its wing or croaks above the arid waste, not even a cricket chirps in the ashen herbage that vainly struggles with the sand.

Here many a traveler has met his doom. Entering this Valley of Death he has wandered on without any landmark to guide save the illusive mountains that ever retreat as they are approached, without tree to shelter, food or water to refresh, till exhausted by the interminable distance, bewildered by the monotony, scared by the awful silence and desolation, he has given up the struggle and fallen to rise no more.

We were not sorry to leave these mountains of despair and emerge into the lower lands that mark the approach to El Paso.

February 23d we reached El Paso, the last town in New Mexico, the last under the protection of the United States flag. Here Mr. David McKenzie met us. He was formerly of the Central Vermont railroad, but is now General Superintendent of the Mexican Central. Upon his shoulders rests almost the entire responsibility of that gigantic work, one thousand two hundred and twenty-four miles in length. His services are justly prized by the owners of the property, for they are characterized by integrity, efficiency, firmness and courage. He has also won the respect of the officials under him, and of the government authorities; not an easy task, but Mr. McKenzie has developed all the requisite qualities.

He received us with generous cordiality, and as he was on the monthly tour of inspection put the train at our service, thus giving us unusual facilities for visiting the large cities and other places of interest on our way to the terminus of the road, the City of Mexico.

El Paso of Texas, although only five years old, boasts of five or six thousand inhabitants, mule cars on the principal streets, electric lights, gambling and drinking houses, and various other modern improvements. The roads, however, are unpaved and sandy, the streets irregular, the whole place having the unfinished look of frontier towns in general. We took a carriage and made a tour of the town, then crossed the sullen Rio Grande, that here cuts its way through the Rockies, giving the place its name — *The Pass.* We were now in the republic of Mexico, in the old town of El Paso del Norte. Here, for the first time, we realized our great distance from home and the novelty of our situation. We were in a foreign land, all our surroundings were changed. We saw Aztecs or peons, as the native Mexicans are called. Their dress was white cotton trousers, woolen blankets, called sarapes, wrapped around their shoulders, and broad-brimmed hats with high conical crowns; the houses and walls were of adobe (sun-dried blocks of mud), one story high, with a single grated window in front, doors in the rear opening into courts or apologies therefor in shape of dirty yards, cactus plants fringing the adobe walls or hedging the gardens; donkeys, called buros, laden with hay, faggots and all kinds of freight on their backs or in great panniers. Here we saw a peach tree in full bloom (February 23), also unfamiliar Spanish and Mexican signs over business places. Perhaps the most startling one was "JESUS C. DOBIE, Liquor Dealer."

We dragged through the sand about two miles to the vineyard of Dr. Alexander, formerly of Texas, who settled in this place many years ago with his wife and daughter. The house is of adobe, one story high, with a veranda taken from the middle of the building, supported by white pillars. Mrs. Alexander, who was on this interior porch with her daughter, gave us hospitable welcome and offered us seats. She is a large, handsome person, with resolution and courage—supposed to be a monopoly of the other sex—stamped on every lineament and patent in every motion. Her character does not belie her appearance. She superintends the plantation, and if the peon laborers are insubordinate she draws her revolver and speedily brings them to terms. If the doctor is absent she receives patients and ministers to their ailments with the same fearlessness. Nevertheless, in voice, features and manner she is feminine and ladylike, and the anxiety she expressed for the welfare of her husband, who is now in Boston on business, proves her a devoted wife.

At a motion from the mother the younger lady went out and presently returned with a tray of glasses well filled with the celebrated Mission wine, entirely free from alcoholic mixture, made from a grape introduced into this country by the Spanish monks.

I partook of this beverage to the extent of a few drops, out of compliment to the hostess; but this being in violation of both principle and taste, I returned the still unemptied glass.

After a few minutes of pleasant conversation we perceived that the sun had set, and remembering that the twilight is very brief in a semi-tropical latitude, we regretfully made our adieus.

Chapter Two.

IN ANCIENT AZTLAN.

NOVEL SCENERY—CHIHUAHUA—A SILVER MILL—BUROS—PRIMITIVE AGRICULTURAL IMPLEMENTS—THE CATHEDRAL—A DWELLING HOUSE—EARLY VEGETATION—JIMINEZ—A TOBACCO PORT—A SILVER CITY.

WE remained all night in our car at El Paso, and in the morning, February 24, resumed our journey by Mr. McKenzie's special train. All day the same barren plains, flanked by distant mountains and nearer sand hills, meet the eye; the same herds of cattle, rancheros, (farm houses) adobe buildings, and occasionally a hut built into a sand bank. We passed one pyramidal hill where four of the engineers employed in the construction of this road met their death at the hands of the bloody Apaches, and also a spring where forty Mexicans were decoyed and mercilessly shot by the same fierce savages. These deadly Indians should receive the treatment accorded to wolves and tigers, the human element rendering them more dangerous because more cunning than wild beasts, as the murder of many men and innocent women abundantly proves.

During this day's ride, among other strange formations, we passed a famous mountain similar to the Palisades of the Hudson and the Giant's Causeway of Ireland, which bears the name of Organ Mountain, though its bent and twisted pipes of collossal proportions suggest discord rather than harmony, when the fierce tempest "strikes his thunder harp" of stone. We passed the battlefield of Sacramento, and also the place where, during the war with Mexico, Gen. Donahue and seven hundred and fifty men, who had marched from St. Louis through this wilderness, met and repulsed the Mexican army, leaving double that number of the enemy dead upon the field, with loss of only one of our men.

At 3.30 p. m. we came to the station of Chihuahua, a mile and a half from the city. From this point our car first ran up to the mill of the silver mine St. Eulalia, owned principally by Mr. Cheney, of Boston, and Mr. A. H. Barney, of New York. There we witnessed the processes of crushing, grinding and separating the precious ore. The din of twenty crushing stamps, the hiss of the engine, the noisy complaint of the ore torn from its silver soul, the rush of water and the rattle of the shoveled mass, made a pandemonium to uninitiated ears. I left the mill with the conviction that wealth taken gently from mother earth in vegetable products is vastly more desirable than such galore. There, as in so many other places, the superintendent told us of the wonders of wealth the mine would produce at some future day; "but just at present the ore is poor, changes must be made, expenses are heavy, returns are small." The same *ignus fatuus* that lures so many men to disappointment and poverty.

But the great event of this day was a visit to the ancient city of Chihuahua, once boasting one hundred thousand inhabitants, but now reduced to a fifth of that number. Here, as in all Mexican cities, are seen adobe houses with flat mud roofs, grated windows in front, doors in the rear opening into courts that are entered by side alleys. The low stories suggest earthquakes; the fortified appearance of the houses, treachery and theft. Again we see droves of diminutive buros with loaded panniers of fire-wood larger than their bodies. The wood is cut in the mountains seven or eight miles distant, the donkeys are driven the whole day without food or water, and at night are turned out on the plain to satisfy hunger and fatigue as best they can, till the light of another day calls them to labor. Yet, with all this neglect and hardship, they are patient, dutiful and true, far higher in the moral scale than the lazy, treacherous persons who drive them.

Here we saw pairs of oxen, not yokes, for in place of yokes the draft was sustained by a strip of wood lashed to the head and horns of the useful brutes. Three or four pairs in one team were harnessed to a clumsy wagon with a high rack of poles and enormous wooden wheels, innocent of a particle of iron. It is a constant source of wonder to the beholder that these huge, rickety, unsteady wheels do not crush in or spread apart.

We drove first to the Cathedral, an imposing edifice, bearing date 1638, built when New England was for most part a howling wilderness. Like most Mexican public buildings, it was of rough stone covered with plaster on the main walls, but finished and decorated with handsome stone carvings. The front is ornamented with pillars, niches, statues and scroll work, in imitation of European cathedrals, but like all imitations, it is an exaggeration and failure almost sacrilegious. The statues, ill-proportioned and cadaverous, have been rendered still more hideous by misapplied paint. The interior, which was intended to be sublime, is still more faulty, with exception of the arches and altar front, which are really fine. The images were most disreputable; dropsical and deformed limbs were attached to time-stained, weazen-faced figures, and the Virgin, adorned with a sailor hat and a fashionable blue silk dress, trimmed with coarse cotton lace, was among the noticeable incongruities. Yet here on the hard stone knelt solemn worshippers, unburdening their sin-laden, sorrowful hearts, and no doubt receiving the answer of peace.

How diverse the form and exhibition of religious sentiment—yet the need of all humanity is one, deliverance from the bondage of flesh, assertion of the power of spirit.

We left the church and visited a banking house, with a dwelling attached, in process of construction by an American contractor. This was the first Mexican tenement proper we had visited, and the interior arrangement quite charmed us. A short hall on one side leads into a court beautifully paved, open to the sky, surmounted by a gallery which is supported on arches and white pillars. A broad marble staircase leads to the second story and a corridor surrounding the court, which opens into the family rooms. The general effect was so enchanting that we began to plan an adaptation of these ideas to our own dwellings, but the remembrance of a northern blizzard, a zero cold wave, with a heavy fall of snow rushing into the open court, filling stone corridors and galleries, caused a sudden revulsion of feeling, our teeth chattered and our lips were dumb. Moorish architecture and Vermont climate, we fear, are irreconcilable. Still, we are all more or less Spanish proprietors, and, while we can dream will never relinquish possession of our castles in Spain.

We drove through the ancient Alameda, laid out on the banks of the river, at this season a mere bed of sand. A double row of dying willows, uninviting stone benches and broken adobe walls mark the spot where, in the palmy days of Chihuahua, horses pranced and carriages rumbled, while stately pedestrians pursued their way along the shady walks.

But the glory has departed; Ichabod is stamped upon the melancholy scene, impressing the beholder with the ever repeated, ever unheeded lesson, "These, too, must pass away!"

As we drove along our guide pointed out the prison where Hidalgo, the liberator priest of Mexico, spent the last night of his life, and also the place of his execution. Now a monument, unavailing, marks the spot. Alas, that so many of earth's noblest and best should have worn only the martyr's crown, while some base usurper wields the sceptre that should have been their own.

But let us remember that our present state is simply a world of actions leading to a world of consequences, and although the bandage upon the eyes of Justice conceals from mortals the direction of her stern, impartial glance, it is only a loosely folded transparent veil, which does not obstruct her vision. She weighs deliberately, adjusts the scales with exactness, and Time stands ready to tip the beam as Justice may dictate.

"An hour cometh that will requite all."

We saw a grand old stone aqueduct, built on arches by the Spaniards, and the modern one, better made, that brings water from a mountain seven or eight miles distant. This abundant supply runs in small waterways along the streets, dispensing life and health to man, beast and vegetation.

The water supply is the great desideratum in this country, where rain is unknown for half the year, a want which we can hardly realize who live in a land of springs, streams and frequent showers.

The early wheat showed green in the broad fields, the trees smiled and sparkled under the caress of spring, the cactus towered upon the wall, the native women peered through the iron lattices at the strangers, children played in the courts after the thoughtless manner of all young creatures, men wrapped in gay sarapes leaned against the walls, or squatted on the ground in the sunshine. All was so novel and seductive we fain would linger; but the sun, which waits not for man's pleasure or hastens for his pain, sank in the west, and remembering the brevity of the twilight, we turned our reluctant footsteps to our home in the Bellevue car.

Next day, February 25th, we stopped half an hour at Jiminez, where we saw the great prairie schooners, as freight wagons are called; groups of natives standing listlessly round the station, the men wearing sarapes and the women robosas, as the universal wraps over the shoulders are called. We visited the railroad warehouse, where, among other freight, was the monthly receipt of thirty tons of cigars. What a waste of money—no, that is a trifle—what a waste of nerve and vitality is implied by the annual consumption of three hundred and sixty tons of cigars in one section of the republic of Mexico.

On the morning of February 26th we reached the highest point of the Zacatecas Mountains, eight thousand and forty-four feet above the sea. The day was fair, the sky cloudless—indeed, we were above ordinary cloud-land; the mountains justified the adjective, sapphire. After an ascent of eighteen miles up a grade of seventy-eight feet to the mile, with sharp curves on the edge of steep precipices, we came to the wonderful city Zacatecas, seventy-five thousand inhabitants, lying among silver hills seven or eight thousand feet above the sea. Here are the richest silver mines in Mexico; in 1881 a sum exceeding five millions of dollars was taken out. The hills that surround the city are pierced in hundreds of places, and from our railroad eyrie we could see the doomed horses treading the harsh ore charged with deadly chemicals. The flat roofs of the houses were beneath us, all of adobe mud, with apertures in the rough cornices to drain the infrequent showers.

The vegetable growths at this high altitude are wonderful—huge cacti, yuccas and strange evergreens.

The curves and grades over these mountains are fearful: the deep cuts are through volcanic deposits; everywhere lava is to be seen. All the earth and rock taken out in construction was carried away upon the backs of men. In many places it was impossible to use even the sure-footed buro.

Chapter Three.

ON THE LINE OF THE MEXICAN CENTRAL RAILROAD.

NATURAL HOT BATHS AND LAUNDRIES—MEXICAN FRUITS—PULQUE—DISHONEST TRAITS—SCENES IN A STRANGE CITY—MANSIONS OF MEXICAN GRANDEES—GUANAJUATA MARBLE—A MEXICAN IDEAL HOME—REDUCTION WORKS—A TRAGIC EVENT.

WE also stopped this day at the city of Agua Calientes, which takes its name from a remarkable hot spring. The water is brought a mile in a large open aqueduct, where the populace bathe and do their washing. We visited the bath buildings, which are spacious and handsome, as usual of stone covered with plaster, durable in this dry climate. A long arched corridor opens into the bath rooms; floors, ceilings, tubs are of stone. The swimming baths are large tanks of stone enclosed in high walls, but open to the sky. Here an abundant supply of warm water, clear as crystal, rushes in after its journey of a mile under ground. It looked so inviting that we longed for a plunge, but our limited stay forbade such a luxury.

A large building, at right angles with the baths, is devoted to laundry purposes. The hot water is conducted into a long reservoir, at the base of which, under an arched corridor, stone-wash tubs are placed about two and a half feet above the ground. Before these tubs stood women with soap and soiled linen, which they beat and rubbed in primitive fashion. I counted twenty-four of these convenient wash-tubs. No lifting water in and out, no building of fires, filling of boilers or cleaning of sloppy floors; down in the dark recesses of earth all this labor is performed. No sweltering in summer heat, no shivering in winter cold. I almost envied the natives their beautiful climate and hot spring—but then, there are drawbacks.

In the gardens the trees were in full leaf; poppies, marigolds and other flowers were in blossom (February 26), the sun was warm as in summer; our parasols were in requisition.

Upon return to the depot we met the usual motley crowd. They offered the fruits of the country for sale, and we purchased for a trifle, cocoanuts, maumees, grenidetas, prickly pears, oranges, citrons, etc. Surely we are approaching the tropics.

The grenidetas resemble a small spherical gourd; the pulp is a soft jelly-like mass, grey, with small black seeds, but juicy and delicious. Another fruit, met with later, is the sapote, like a green tomato filled with blackberry jam without the seeds; still another, the cherimoya (the spelling may not be correct), is green and ill-favored, but contains within a rich white substance, very delicious and refreshing. Both these last mentioned fruits are eaten with a spoon.

I have tasted the far-famed pulque. This drink, harmless when fresh, disgusting after fermentation has well set in, and intoxicating when old, resembles in taste and color thin yeast, or some say, stale buttermilk. It is made from the maguey or agave, our century plant. The crown of the plant is cut out at a certain age and the cup thus formed fills with the juice of the plant, which is carefully dipped out; some plants produce several pints. Thousands of acres are devoted to the cultivation of the maguey plants, which grow to great size in this country.

The Mexicans, who are very fond of the drink, have an adage which runs thus:

> "Know ye not pulque,
> That liquor divine!
> Angels in heaven
> Prefer it to wine."

If this be true, angels must have a very gross taste, and Paradise must produce grapes of wretched quality.

At our first stopping place, Silao, we saw the mounted guards of Wells, Fargo & Co. We were in a land where thieves and robbers abound. Thieving is as common as lying, and that is the rule, not the exception. The very spikes are stolen from the railroad tracks, the links and pins from the couplers; the watchmen are sometimes the culprits. We are warned not to leave the open door of our car unwatched for a moment. At every stopping place a crowd of lazy peons, in slouch hats and gay blankets, throng the platforms of our car and peer through the doors and windows, ready to seize anything they can reach. They come close and inspect our dress and jewelry. I counted nearly twenty last night just before the car door, ready to take advantage of the least relaxation of vigilance.

From Silao we ran up to Marfil, thirteen miles, and there took the tramway for Guanajuata, a city which, like Zacatecas, lies high up among silver hills. This proved to be a very interesting visit. The valley, or rather ravine, is so deep and narrow that many of the buildings hang upon the hillsides; some of the streets are hundreds of feet almost directly above others. It is a very busy city, second only to Zacatecas in the production of silver. Large droves of laden buros, sometimes fifty in a drove, crowd the steep, stony streets, conveying merchandise of every description. The patience and fidelity of these diminutive animals are a growing wonder. It cannot be that such virtues are annihilated when breath leaves the worn-out frame.

We went first to the plazza or park, refreshingly bright with tropical trees; thence to the residence of the president of the Tramway Company. We were under the escort of one of the officials, and as the family were absent we were allowed to climb the stone stairways, through lofty corridors and chambers, till the top of the house was reached, where a bird's-eye view of this strange city was obtained.

After descending we walked up the street to the grand plazza, which is flanked on the sides by terraced gardens and handsome houses, and on to the residences of ex-President Gonzales and ex-Governor

Chico. These places were a surprise and delight, oases in the dusty, stony city. That of President Gonzales is a long, low white building, with arched windows and broad stone walks, the grounds adorned with shrubs, trees and plants. It is above the street, on a terrace, in front of which is an artificial pond or tank, where just then a fine horse was swimming. Directly behind this mansion is a strangely formed, dark, rocky mountain, and at the moment a great white cloud lay behind it, towering up into the azure sky. As we walked along the street we passed a point where a heavy clump of tall shivering trees parted, disclosing the mansion lying against the dark mountain resting against the cloud—a startling effect, never to be forgotten.

The adjoining grounds of ex-Governor Chico are similar to those of Gonzales. Here we were admitted. The gardens seemed like enchantment to our northern eyes, so recently resting on a waste of snow. Novel and familiar plants met the eye. The gardener gathered and presented us violets, cape jessamines, carnations and roses, but pointed out with greatest pride a few fine pansies growing in pots.

While standing in this garden a crisp, cool little breeze, such as had before excited our surprise, came dancing down from the hills or clouds, or heaven, whirling and tossing about leaves, flowers and garments, everything in its way, more like an electric current, a spirit, or some celestial messenger which, roaming along the confines of cloud-land, had dropped to earth, and after a moment of confusion discovered its gross surroundings and bounded away to regain its native element. Even as we drank in the sweet influence it was gone.

In the construction of the more elegant buildings of Guanajuata there is a peculiar marble used that impressed us much as did the celestial breezes. It is of a pale atmospheric green, clouded in beautiful shades. It takes a high polish, and when placed does not convey the slightest suggestion of weight. A church of this marble would seem indeed a spiritual temple, or the jasper walls of St. John's vision.

After leaving this part of the city we went, by invitation, to the residence of Signor Ybarando, manager of the Branch National Bank. He is a very accomplished gentleman, who thinks so highly of our institutions that he sent his children to the United States to lay the foundation of their education. He received us with the utmost cordiality, but excused the absence of his wife, who is ill from some affection of the brain. The lady is said to be one of the most beautiful and highly cultivated women in Mexico, as well as a person of great courage and strength of character. Her three children were presented to us, two sons and a daughter. Their manners were as perfect as their faces were beautiful, being quiet, dignified and self-possessed.

We saw in possession of these happy young people one of the little black dogs for which the city of Chihuahua is celebrated, which I forgot to mention in my last letter. The wonderfully diminutive creatures are soft, glossy and black. They are greatly prized by natives and foreigners, sometimes bringing as much as two hundred dollars each. It is said they can not be bred anywhere but in Chihuahua.

The drawing-rooms of this house were furnished in American styles; the dining room similar to ours. The table was hospitably spread in our honor with native fruits and sweetmeats. Signor Ybarando asked me if I would like to see a Mexican kitchen, and guided us to a small room about eight by ten, one entire side of which was occupied by a long range of stone, in which were five or six openings; beneath each of these was a charcoal burner fed from a small arch in front of the range. There was no chimney—there is not one in Mexico—but a great stone hood surmounted the range, at the highest point of which an opening permitted the egress of the fumes.

It was time for us to leave; we went into the corridor above stairs; it was open to the blue sky; growing plants and singing birds adorned it; all was so peaceful and lovely we were loth to depart; but other scenes awaited us, and returning the usual "thousand thanks," we made our adieus.

We next visited the reduction works of a hacienda near by. The polite superintendent made us welcome, and, gallantly offering me his arm, led the way through numerous mills, where the patient, blindfold mules were grinding silver ore. We then passed to enormous vats, one or two hundred feet long, where the patient brutes were treading out the silver and their wretched lives at the same time. The pulverized ore is mixed with vitrol, quicksilver and water, to the consistence of thick mud. Round and round, in this horrible slush, the poor mules are driven, while the chemicals do the work of disintegration upon the ore and the feet of the animals; and when the silver has settled, by its greater weight, the refuse is washed away. The metals then go into retorts; the quicksilver is sublimated by heat, and the precious silver run into ingots.

With many thanks to the superintendent for his courtesy we took leave and went through the markets, certainly not characterized by neatness. New potatoes, pepper and beans were the chief commodities on sale at this late hour.

Here we saw what before had attracted our attention—a primitive way of obtaining water, the scarcest article, it would seem, in this arid land from October to June. Water carriers perambulate every street, with jars about four feet long and about a foot in diameter, strapped on their backs with leathern thongs. Crowds of women and children stand ready with jars and pitchers to receive the precious fluid, without which the processes of housekeeping as well as of life must cease. Thus year after year and generation after generation, tens of thousands live upon a scanty dole that would in our favored land scarcely serve to flush a single drain. It is a saying among Mexicans that " they climb for their water and dig for their wood "—the former being generally obtained from springs high up in the mountains, and the wood being mostly the gnarly roots of the musquit, a shrub or tree that flourishes on the arid plains.

At three p. m. we were again on our way to the City of Mexico, fragments of scripture floating through the brain:

"Oh, thou that dwellest in the clefts of the rocks, that holdest the heights of the hills, though thou shouldst make thy nest as high as the eagle, I will bring thee down from thence, saith the Lord God."

Shortly after we were at Guanajuata a strange and dreadful event took place. Upon a high mountain over the city, on a nearly inaccessible height, is to be seen, relieved against the sky, a shrine to the Virgin Mary. To this place penitents creep, sometimes on their knees, in hope of expiating their sins. It was stated in the newspapers that the day subsequent to our visit, a man and a woman, apparently in the higher walks of life, toiled up the rugged mountain, and, after standing motionless a few minutes, hurled themselves down the awful precipice and were dashed to pieces on the rocks below. Their bodies were mangled past hope of recognition. They were strangers, and there was not the slightest clue to the motive that prompted such an awful suicide.

Chapter Four.

THE CITY OF MEXICO.

ANCIENT TENOCHTITLAN—SUMMER—FLOWERS—SUNDAY A GALA DAY—HOTEL ITERBIDE—SIGHT-SEEING—THE CATHEDRAL—THE WATER GAUGE—HALL OF ANTIQUITIES—MUSEUM—THE HELODERMA—SERPENTS AND LIZARDS—GAUDELOUPE—AZTEC MONUMENTS.

> "Thou art beautiful,
> Queen of the Valley, thou art beautiful!
> Thy walls like silver sparkle in the sun,
> Melodious wave thy groves, thy garden sweets
> Enrich the pleasant air; upon the lakes
> Lie the long shadows of thy towers, and high
> In heaven thy temple pyramids arise
> Against the clear, blue sky."

FEBRUARY 28th, at 8.25 p. m., we reached the City of Mexico, after a terrific ride over the Lena Mountains at the height of eight thousand one hundred and thirty-two feet. We here experienced in a greater degree than we had previously, the effects of high altitude: short breath, headache, dizziness, buzzing in the ears, nose-bleed and general discomfort; the strongest in our party succumbed.

The grated barriers of the railroad station were among the first novelties that attracted our attention; precaution against lawless violence is everywhere seen. Nominally a republic, there is really no self-government in Mexico; the strong arm of force is necessary; liberty and license are incompatible.

The gentlemen of our party went into the city to make arrangements for our reception, while we strolled upon the ample platform. The sun shone warm; people remarked: "It will be a hot day." The tall, green trees stood motionless against an unclouded sky, the birds sang merrily in the branches—the weather was June at her best. Just then a messenger came with a telegram from Vermont: "Weather cold and blustering." It hardly seemed possible!

In a few minutes a mule cart drove up for our baggage, and a coach for ourselves. In the latter were flowers sent by kind friends as a welcome. I doubt if a two-bushel basket would have held the enormous bouquets. We entered the carriage loaded with flowers, and one of our party remarked that she felt like a prima donna leaving the theatre after an opera triumph. As we tore through the streets (our coachman was a Jehu) novel scenes met the eye at every turn. No Sabbath stillness; the day of sacred rest is here a holiday, a day for license, a day of sport; then thieves ply their vocation most successfully, for everybody is out, and the church, with its kneeling worshippers, is a most convenient place for their operations. The entire population seemed to be in the streets; Mexicans on horseback, with the typical sombrero (slouched hat) gay jacket and light-colored pantaloons, all profusely trimmed with gold and silver lace; carriages with handsomely dressed ladies, wearing black lace mantillas—not bonnets—on their heads ; and pedestrians in gay attire ; public gardens filled with tropical plants ; houses with grated windows, open shops, walled courts, donkeys with heavy loads, business wagons creaking with freight, all passed by us in a pageant, under the bluest of skies and brightest of suns. The pavement was rough, and the guardian of the horses delighted in a furious gait and a zigzag course. I verily believe he crossed the tramway twenty-five times before we reached our destination.

The Hotel Iterbide, where we stopped, an enormous building, like most of those in Mexico, is of stone overlaid with plaster and highly ornamented with stucco work. The large courts are as usual open to the cloudless sky, the long, intricate passages and stone stairways seem interminable to the newly-arrived and puzzled guest. It was originally built for Gen. Iterbide, once ruler of Mexico, a man with only one hand, but so grasping and dishonest, it is said, if he had possessed the usual complement of fingers nothing would have been left in the republic that did not belong to him.

The rooms in this pretentious building are small and ill-furnished ; water and candles are the only extras provided—everything else must be separately paid for, yet the average expense is low. The chambermaids are men, Mexican peons ; the restaurant is very unsatisfactory. We took baths, which are admirably arranged, and dined at the hotel. Thinking to better our table we went next morning to "The

Concordia," another hotel. A large roll, so hard that literally I could not break it, a thin, white, oily wafer, called butter, a cup of coffee composed mostly of milk, and a hard-done omelette was the bill of fare.

A kind friend called and offered himself as guide and interpreter, and after breakfast we began our exploration of the city. And here, I would say, it must be remembered that in this delightful climate there is no "postponement on account of the weather," and little variation in thermometer or barometer during the entire year; the sun is almost always shining, and even in the rainy season there is only a shower every day. The air is delightful, but the altitude is so great that strangers get out of breath with slight exertion; persons newly arrived sometimes faint ascending stairs. The people thronging the thoroughfares are of three classes: First, the descendants of the Spaniards, generally the wealthiest and most highly educated, the grandees of the nation; second, the peons, or descendants of the native Aztecs; and, lastly, Indians, nomads of various tribes, very low in the scale of intelligence, so low that some of them come into the city naked savages. These are seized by officials appointed for the purpose and clothed with a blanket at government expense.

We first visited the cathedral, a grand, highly ornate edifice, more magnificent and gorgeous within than those in Europe, although the proportions and architecture do not equal the marvels of the East, there is a greater amount of gilded carving, images, banners and frescoes.

Morning service was in progress, conducted by different priests in various parts of the building at the same time. Some of the congregations were very large, all kneeling or standing, no seats being used. A magnificent organ sounded at intervals, answered by choirs not so fine. The church is surrounded by a flower garden, and on one side is a large flower market, where at least on Sunday mornings lovers and fond husbands go to select beautiful flowers. Across the street is a plazza, or park, always thronged by a motley crowd, as here is a drinking fountain, and it is in the busiest part of the city. Near the cathedral is a curious and ingenious water gauge, which marks the rise and fall of Lake Texcoco, which nearly surrounds the city at a distance of nine miles. Its level is but slightly below the streets, and sometimes it has overflowed and caused terrible floods in the city. To warn the people in season to prepare for such a cataclysm this register has been invented. It is connected with the lake, and shows the actual height of the water at any given moment.

On the corner opposite the cathedral is the National Museum. We first visited the Hall of Antiquities, where are gathered the few relics of a tremendous prehistoric civilization that Spanish superstition and fanaticism have left for a wondering world.

The Toltec calendar, or astronomical stone, is a huge disc eight or ten feet in diameter, carved with unknown characters, including two serpents. There are also colossal human figures in a recumbent posture, recently discovered in the wilds of Yucatan;

various huge idols in sculptured stone, not unlike the Buddhas of the Orient in posture; the Aztec war god, a horrible monster with skirt of woven rattlesnakes, the heads forming the fringe; three or four colossal figures of the feathered sun serpent; last and most horrible, the great sacrificial stone, eight or nine feet in diameter and five or six feet in thickness from the ground. The whole top and sides are covered with peculiar designs, and in the center of the flat surface is a place hollowed out to receive the shoulders of the victim, from which a channel or gutter leads to the outer edge to permit the flow of blood. Here, it is said, sixty thousand human beings have been immolated, a mournful relic of peoples and nations who believed that "without the shedding of blood there is no remission of sin," but who understood not the hidden, spiritual meaning of that tremendous truth.

Other halls of the museum are filled with products of different Mexican provinces; minerals, marbles, fossils, wares, preserved beasts, monstrosities, insects and reptiles. Among these last was a horrible lizard, peculiar to the Healey River, called the Gela Monster. The specimen was the color of gray stone, two feet in length, though sometimes it is yellow with black spots, and five feet long. Sharp, irregular spines run along the back, and under its vicious jaws is a large bag or pouch, from which, it is said, this horror of nature can expel a gas so deadly that any living creature will swoon upon inhaling it. In an El Paso journal of March 25th I found the following account of the Heloderma or Gela Monster: "It is the only venomous lizard in the world, so far as is known, and is confined to Mexico, Lower California and Arizona. The poison comes from glands in the mouth, and the teeth are channeled to accelerate its passage into the wound. Brandy and whiskey, often efficacious in rattlesnake poison, have no effect on the virus of this lizard, perhaps because the physiological action is so different. The snake bite paralyzes the respiratory centre, the poison of the Gela Monster paralyzes the heart. I saw a man killed by a heloderma under most distressing circumstances. A large one, four or five feet long, had been captured and tied to a post. A drunken man began to torment it, saying he did not believe it to be venomous. Those standing around warned him and forcibly took him away several times, but he returned and thrust his hand into the reptile's mouth. He was sober in a moment; sharp pains and swelling of the arm ensued immediately; he went into the most terrible convulsions, and died on the spot where he fell, in less than an hour, among a group of pale men who were utterly powerless to give him relief."

As this description of the Heloderma elicited considerable attention and inquiry at the time it first appeared in print, our readers may be interested in the following account which is taken from the New York Tribune just as this chapter goes to press:

FURIOUS BATTLE BETWEEN TWO REPTILES BELONGING TO THE FISH COMMISSION.

WASHINGTON, Oct. 29.—A rare combat took place this afternoon in a building occupied by the Fish Commission, between the newly-arrived "monster" from the Gila River in Arizona and a two-year-old alligator from Florida. The lizard is fourteen inches long and about twice the weight of his antagonist. Both reptiles were in a semi-torpid condition, having ceased to take food a week or two ago, and for some purpose they had been removed from their glass cases and placed beside each other upon the stone floor. An attendant inadvertently touched the alligator's tail, and caused him to move sluggishly onward a few inches, when he came in contact with the blunt nose of the lizard. The snaky eyes of the lizard lighted up; his black lips opened wide, and his jaws closed with a snap upon the fore paw of the alligator. The prisoner made for a time a gallant fight for liberty and life. His movements were marvelously quick, and his jaws closed a dozen times in quick succession upon the mailed head of his assailant. He soon, however, became exhausted, and moaning like a suffering child, lapsed into quietude.

The attendants sought by a variety of means to release the wretched alligator, but were compelled to be extremely careful in handling the venomous "monster." He was seized by the tail and held up in the air; taken by his bloated neck and choked severely; plunged under water, and maltreated in other ways, but to no purpose. Then sharp wires were thrust into his nose, and finally a large trowel was thrust into his mouth; but such was the force of his grasp that the steel blade, though considerably bent in the effort, failed to release the imprisoned paw. Then the pair were replaced in the glass case which had been occupied by the lizard, and again the alligator renewed his struggles, thrashing his enemy with his tail and snapping at him with his jaws. In his struggles he had dislocated his shoulder, and the imprisoned limb became limp and powerless. At last the trowel was again introduced into the lizard's mouth, and probably made a severe wound in some tender part. Bubbles of grayish slime were exuded from the mouth and nostrils, and finally the jaws slowly opened. Even then it was a work of several minutes to disengage the hooked fangs from the wounded paw. The combatants were placed in their separate cages, the lizard lapping his thick black lips with his greenish forked tongue, while the alligator closed his eyes, probably to die of the venom.

That mere natural influence, even in the desert wastes of Mexico and Arizona, should produce such an appalling creature is almost incomprehensible. It certainly seems as if the "l" in its name should be a double letter.

The rattlesnake and heloderma are mortal foes, and their battles, sometimes witnessed by hunters, are among the most terrible sights in nature. Other serpents, also scorpions abound in Mexico. At Durango the latter are a frightful pest. Their sting is invariably fatal to children—sometimes proving so in a few minutes. Though the government has placed a bounty on their heads and as many as one hundred thousand are killed in a year, they cannot be exterminated. It is said the birds of Mexico never sing, but I think that true only of those in captivity.

After leaving the museum, we took the tramway to the church of Gaudeloupe, three miles distant. Just as the train started, the cathedral bell tolled the midday hour. A more solemn, musical, deep-toned bell I have never heard. At the sound of the bell all the natives uncover their heads till the reverberation passes away.

The Church of the Virgin of Gaudeloupe is a magnificent structure, founded upon the spot indicated by an apparition of the Virgin Mary. The command to build the church in this place was given to a peasant boy, and in token of authenticity, it is said, she impressed her picture upon his apron. We saw the veritable apron in a glass case at the museum. If it is a true portrait the Virgin does not come up to our ideal in beauty or spirituality.

The great effigy over the altar of this church is, according to our ideas, a blasphemy. Upon an immense guilt triangle are the sitting images of an old man and a young one; over the group hovers a dove; these are intended to represent the Trinity. The careless and irreverent use of things considered by us too sacred to be mentioned without the utmost solemnity, is frequent and shocking. One of our friends heard a man say to his servant, "Jesus, come here and black my boots!"

The choir of Gaudeloupe is superb, above anything we have previously seen. Not even the carving of the temptation scene in Antwerp equals that in the choir of Gaudeloupe. We counted thirty-seven panels in the half-circle, and under them a double row of seats, admirably carved in rosewood, each relief representing a different sacred scene. These marvels of art are highly polished, and are almost black with age.

The numerous and extended railings in the main body of the church are of solid silver, placed there at a cost of seven millions of dollars. Upon leaving the church we saw a large pile of crutches, which we were told had been left by invalids after miraculous cures; these were from sizes that would fit a giant to one about a foot long—the last left there no doubt by a decrepit doll.

We entered the small but beautiful chapel, built over the muddy spring which is supposed to effect these sudden and miraculous cures. At this time, and I suppose it is thus always, a throng of ragged, wretched peasants lingered in the area, bearing pitchers and jars filled with the muddy water of the well.

Going and coming from Gaudeloupe, a fine view of the extinct volcano Popacatapelt is often obtained, but owing to a hazy condition of the atmosphere we had only the imperfect outline. In this ride, however, we passed between some curious Aztec monuments, fifteen or twenty feet high, uniform in size and shape, placed at equal distances along the sides of the highway: we also left and entered the city through a gateway of the wall that encloses it.

We dined this day, and every other of our stay in Mexico, at the Café Anglais, the least exceptionable restaurant in the city. Many of the dishes were familiar, but those which required boiling were conspicuous by their absence, as evaporation in that rarified atmosphere takes place before the requisite heat can be obtained. Frying is substituted, but fried string beans and cauliflower were not to our taste. The place is untidy and noisy, thronged with guests of every nationality. The waiters understand only Spanish, for conquerors always force their language upon the conquered. As an indication of the ethical condition of this city, it may be mentioned that the growing plants in the entry of the Café are wired down to prevent their loss.

After dinner we went out to look for Mexican

curios; opals, strange painted bowls and plaques, feather pictures, wax images covered with a fine web of cloth which preserves but does not disfigure them, shell work, silver and gold jewelry, Aztec relics and pottery, peculiar to different sections of the republic.

We slept at the Iterbide; that is, some of our party slept, but others abandoned their couches to the small aboriginal inhabitants who valiantly and successfully disputed possession with them.

Chapter Five.

THE HALLS OF MONTEZUMA.

A PRIVATE CIRCUS—CHAPULTEPEC—MONUMENTS IN THE ALAMEDA—THE HEIGHTS—HISTORIC PLACES—THE PALACE AT CHAPULTEPEC—RESIDENCE OF THE YSCANDONS—SUPERB FURNITURE—MEXICAN RAILROAD—MOUNTAIN GRANDEUR—ABYSSES—GORGES—THE HOT LANDS.

TUESDAY, March 2d, we had arranged to go early to Chapultepec, the Hill of Grasshoppers. Why so named I have never learned. There certainly is not grass enough on the heights to tempt these insects. Probably it was the totem, or sacred symbol of the Aztecs or Zoltecs, adopted according to custom among the aborigines of America.

> "They painted on the grave posts
> Each the symbol of his household,
> Figures of the bear and reindeer,
> Of the turtle, crane and beaver."

This place of historic fame is a few miles from the city, the seat of the Emperor Maximillian's short-lived grandeur—a fortress captured by Gen. Scott during our war with Mexico—once occupied by the cruel General Cortez—and still more remotely, the site upon which stood the Halls of Montezuma.

The friends who were to accompany us were a little behind time, having had, as they expressed it, "a private circus at their own house early in the morning." The mistress, upon rising earlier than usual, found a strange man in the house, admitted, as it proved, by her confidential servant. The husband, the porter and the police were hastily summoned and the culprits were taken to prison. There is absolutely no reliance to be placed on these people. This is the testimony of every foreigner we have met.

We made the trip to Chapultepec in carriages, passing along the Alameda, or grand driveway and promenade, beautifully laid out with trees, walks, fountains and stands for music. In the boulevard leading to Chapultepec are two very fine monuments, one to Columbus and another to Montezuma—this latter a tardy honor bestowed upon a brave, unfortunate monarch, defeated, dethroned, tortured and finally murdered by perfidous Spanish invaders moved by the greed for gold. Our blood boils with indignation as we remember the abuse of generous hospitality, the cruel injustice, the implacable exercise of wanton power exerted by the Spaniards. What scenes of carnage and unavailing sacrifice, what mortal agonies, what groans of despair have been witnessed by these calm skies and cold mountains! Is there a just avenger who notes the affairs of men? Doubt not—"Justice and truth will in the end certainly prevail, and if at times it seems otherwise, it is because we see the middle and not the end." "The mills of the gods grind slowly, but they grind exceedingly small." "Every man shall receive according to the deeds done in the body, whether they are good or whether they are bad."

We soon reached the magnificent height, now crowned by a palace and fortress, and used by the government as a military school. A winding road, bordered with trees placed there through the munificence of the unhappy queen Carlotta, leads up to the citadel. A wonderful view is presented from the walls; a verdant plain, a grand range of mountains, over which towers the snow-clad giant Popocatapetl, seventeen thousand five hundred feet high—a third of a mile higher than Mont Blanc. Near him lies Ixtacihuatl (the woman in white) another snowy volcano, which bears resemblance to a woman in a recumbent posture, covered with a white shroud. An interesting legend is that this mountain was the wife of the giant Popocatapetl; in a moment of jealous rage he struck her dead, and for ages afterward gave vent to grief and remorse in awful volcanic throes and storms of ashes and fire.

We saw, at this most interesting place, the slight monument that marks the battlefield of Moline del Rey, where Gen. Winfield Scott gained a victory over the Mexican army; also the place where he stormed and carried the heights; where Gen. Ransom fell, for whom our St. Albans guards were named. In rear of the fortress a lofty monument honors "The memory of Mexican cadets who fell by the hands of American invaders."

The palace now in process of reconstruction we

were not allowed to enter. A more fortunate visitor describes it thus:

"The woodwork and upholstering of the east wing alone cost two hundred thousand dollars. The frescoing was executed by a pupil of Meissonier. Upon the roof is a beautiful garden of flowers and fountains. The gates are carved and ornamented in bronze. The woodwork of the president's room is ebony and gold. The bath-room is a grotto with a floor of marble mosaics, the walls of French tiles. The floor of the card-room is a parquet of rare woods, the walls are of Cordova leather, with gold and satin panels, and red velvet borders. The parlor is a fairy creation. The wood work is finished with satin panels, marble borders and gold flowers. The walls are covered with satin damask, relieved by blue and gold Aubusson borders."

Our guides were youths connected with the military school, who took pleasure in pointing out the halls, dormitories, recitation rooms and stone stairways.

Upon our descent from the citadel we stopped in a grand but melancholy grove of ancient cypress trees, overgrown with long, gray moss. We paced around the giant tree named for the unhappy Montezuma, and found it sixty-three feet in circumference.

After leaving Chapultepec we visited the residence of the Yscandons, a family perhaps the richest of the Mexican grandees, whose wealth consists of uncounted, unknown millions. A card of admission opened the gates of the grounds and doors of the mansion.

The family being absent, an old servant was our guide.

The grounds are irregularly laid out with graveled and mosaic walks, and ornamented with groves, clumps and rows of trees, beautiful gardens, ponds, swimming baths or tanks for men and horses, fine stables, arbors and a greenhouse in the dome of which a vine had clustered so redundant with rose-colored flowers as to give the impression of a pink cloud. Swans floated in the ponds, scores of rabbits hopped back and forth through their yards and warrens, and in the tall trees some large brown birds kept up a peculiar clamor. There was a miniature house of brick, perfect in all its furniture and appointments, built expressly for the delectation of children; also a private family chapel with stained glass windows, carpets, praying stools and other church furniture, and lighted by a wonderful hanging alabaster lamp.

The exterior of the mansion is handsome, but not pretentious. The interior is a palace. The middle of the building is as usual a court, but in this instance roofed in by a crystal dome; columns of a creamy tint support the encircling galleries and surround the grand drawing-room which occupies the centre on the ground floor. Filling the middle of this magnificent apartment, directly beneath the dome, is a group of life-size figures on a large pedestal, supporting an immense chandelier—all in purest gilt. Near this group is a double divan with vases of artificial flowers upon the broad arms. From this centre we passed between the pillars to wings opening out of the drawing-room, making a unique and spacious apartment, into which has been gathered from all parts of the world rare and costly furniture. Superb cabinets were loaded with Dresden china, the largest and richest designs we have seen, bronzes, Venetian figures, tables and cabinets inlaid with ivory, statues, gilt chairs, sofas and other seats of peculiar construction, clocks, rare and rich, an orchestron, a piano and various works of virtu crowded every apartment. Bay windows were screened off by marble railings and curtained pillars; family portraits of Spanish type and various other pictures hung upon the walls.

One picture was unique and strangely effective. It was a polished stone tablet or panel three feet by two, marked and clouded by some freak of nature as a stormy sky and tempestuous sea. Upon this gloomy background had been painted a ship and group of figures which represented the disciple Peter walking upon the Sea of Galilee to meet his Master. The carpets on this floor were principally Aubusson.

We ascended the marble stairway, which divides into two flights at the first landing and found ourselves in a circular corridor that opens into chambers and dormitories. Here was evidence of the same uncalculating luxury and expense. All the world had paid tribute to the demands of unstinted wealth. The windows of some of these rooms open upon balconies built on the roofs of broad verandas; these are hedged in with metal railings upon which, at regular intervals, life-size bronze figures are placed.

We passed out of this palace through a veranda that particularly impressed me. It was entirely of marble except the floor, which was of encaustic tile. It was about twenty feet by ten in size. In the heavy side walls were windows disclosing a view of the grounds in each direction; the roof was upheld in front by stately pillars. Growing plants, vases, seats and skins of wild beasts on the floor, made the furniture.

As we left this Mexican Eldorado many solemn thoughts surged through the mind; even the Yscandons with all their wealth and power can not purchase exemption from the common lot of humanity. They, too, must suffer disappointment and pain; they, too, must grow old and die. Then, as the sunlight streamed upon the glittering scene, came a verse of Thomas Campbell's address by the Last Man to the fading orb of day:

> "What though beneath thee man puts forth
>   His pride, his pomp and skill,
> And arts that made fire, field and wood
>   The vassals of his will;
> Yet mourn I not thy parted sway,
> Thou dim, discrowned king of day,
>   For all the trophied arts
> And triumphs that beneath thee sprang,
> Healed not a passion nor a pang
>   Entailed on human hearts."

We decided to visit Vera Cruz, on the Gulf of Mexico. It is two hundred and sixty-eight miles from the city of Mexico, over one of the most wonderful railroads in the world, built by English skill and capital at a cost of twenty-seven millions of dollars. The Bellevue, it was feared, was too long to round the sharp curves, as a special car, the "Yellowstone," about the same length, had struck the rocks a few days previous. Mr. Jackson, of the Mexican Central, kindly offered his car, which has often made the trip and is esteemed perfectly safe. Greatly to our satisfaction, Mr. McKenzie arranged to accompany us. Although he has been in this country three years, he had never taken this trip, and it gave him three days of much needed rest from his arduous duties.

March 3rd, at five a. m., we moved out of the Mexican Central depot on our way to Vera Cruz. Miles of agave plantations border the rail and stretch away to the base of the distant Cordilleras. The volcanoes Popocatapetl and The Lady in White appear high above the horizon, like clouds in the sky. At length snow-clad Orizaba—star of the sky—reared his awful front; the mountain walls that encircle this vast plain increased in size and grandeur as we ascend to the highest point, eight thousand feet above sea level. They grew momentarily higher and nearer, till the cook, who is an old traveler on this route, sent in word that we had better dine at once, as all our senses would soon be required for the scenes through which we must pass.

We hardly finished our hasty meal before exclamations of surprise brought us all to the door of the car. Mountains tower up all around us thousands of feet in height, piled Alps on Alps; high, massive walls seem to topple over the narrow path; horrible rents in their sides disclose precipices hundreds of feet beneath us. Our way lies over awful chasms; we are suspended above bottomless abysses; we look down into measureless crevices: we shudder and hold our breath lest even a sigh should throw us off the slender track. We remember the spirit-bridge Chinevet across the abyss Duyhak of Persian mythology, over which the souls of the dead must essay to pass if they would attain the home of the blessed.

We have reached the perilous barranca del Metlac, a gorge a thousand feet deep. Along a narrow shelf of the mountain the engine slowly drags the heavy train up a steep grade, and at the same time around a horse shoe curve, having a radius of only three hundred and fifty-eight feet. To increase the terror of this tremendous pass, the ascending curve includes two iron trestle bridges over yawning chasms, and five tunnels through solid rock.

We see this miracle of engineering in the twilight, made more awful by the shadow of the dark, high mountains piled around in grand confusion. I think the most stolid natures must breathe easier and offer a grateful prayer as they emerge from the gloom of this awful pass and no longer hang in a frail wooden box upon slender wires over a bottomless pit. In the valleys beneath, of which we get occasional glimpses, farms and houses look diminutive as a toy Swiss village. But the double rail holds fast, and we creep slowly from height to height. Long furrows scar the mountain sides; the rock cuts unveil beds of lava thrown from long-forgotten volcanoes.

In fancy's flight we view the terrific majesty of the scene when these mountains were heaving waves on an ocean of fire, and almost shiver as we think of the cold blast that swept over, hardened and petrified their wrinkled crests into these gigantic forms.

We wind round the rocky pass, one moment among the clouds, and anon crossing the hollow plain, again ascending the heights and swinging above a ghastly chasm through which roars a torrent; our lives hang upon a slender trestle; a thread suspends us over an abyss that bears the name of HELL!

The train stops at the station of Orizabe, we walk upon the platform, rejoicing that we are once more on terra firma. We have reached the Tierras Calientes, or Hot Lands. Flowers load the trees and line the pathway. Banana, cocoanut, orange, lemon, palm, coffee and olive trees, the eucalyptus, cullodian, hibiscus, sugar cane, indigo plant, parrots, monkeys, lizards—we see all these. The sun is hot. We are within the tropics.

We reach Vera Cruz at eight o'clock p. m., but swift-footed night precedes us, and it is quite dark; no lingering twilight ekes out the tropical day.

Chapter Six.

VERA CRUZ.

HEAT AND PESTILENCE — ON THE GULF — IN THE DUNGEONS — BRIGHTER SCENES — SUNDAY IN MEXICO — THE BULL FIGHT.

MR. POWELL, Superintendent of the Mole, is waiting at the station with a welcome. The thermometer in his office, at this hour, registers 82°. Mr. Powell is an English gentleman, who has lived twenty years in this fever-stricken country, fought the dreaded foe and come off conqueror. He acknowledged the fearful sanitary condition of the city, but says there is no yellow fever at present, nor will there be until rain falls and the burning sun heats the yellow pools; then the fatal germs ascend and fill the steaming air. The plague rages through July and August, the rainy months, sometimes reproducing itself for more than a year. Here it is seen in its most malignant form; the cause is supposed to exist in a soil saturated with poison from defective drainage.

A night of intense heat followed our arrival, and the morning of March 4th brought in a still warmer day. Our kind friend, Mr. Powell, took us in his barge, with four stout rowers, and for the first time in our lives we floated upon the Gulf of Mexico. The water was calm but for a dead swell (the heel of an old storm) and beautifully blue and transparent. A few sturdy strokes of the oar brought us out into the bay, from which we obtained the best view of this picturesque city, with its glittering white towers, domes and walls, built after the Spanish adaptation of Moorish architecture. Some of the towers are beautifully faced with colored tile. The harbor is a bad one, the waters of the bay being shallow and full of coral reefs, over which the sea breaks with a solemn, warning sound. By Mr. Powell's order, our light boat was brought alongside one of the reefs, and looking down into the transparent water we saw the coral ledges beneath us and felt the beauty of Dr. Holmes' poem, "The Chambered Nautilus":

> "Ours is the venturous bark that flings
> On the summer wind its purple wings
> In gulfs enchanted, where the siren sings
> And coral reefs lie bare,
> Where the cold sea maids rise to sun their streaming hair."

How dreamlike it seemed as we trailed our hands in the waves and watched the pelicans, albatross and sea gulls float around the reefs or stalk through the shoals in unconcerned dignity.

And at this very hour a fierce blizzard swept over our northern home; man and beast were cowering before the fury of an arctic storm.

In the bay of Vera Cruz lies the island of San Luis del Ulua, upon which is a large prison and fortress.

Almost before we are aware of it, our boat passed under the shadow of a Mexican man-of-war and grazed the wall of the fortress. We stepped out and found ourselves on a paved walk leading to the castle; walls, towers, pavements all of coral. We enter the court, the commandant welcomes us, details a captain as guide, and before we can realize the tremendous change which has so unexpectedly come over our surroundings, from summer skies and tropic seas we pass through stony halls, at each step darker, dirtier, more noisome, till we find ourselves among horrible wretches in dungeons, where daylight enters only through a narrow slit in a heavy wall.

It was too dreadful. I begged the guide to take us away, which he did, but only to lead us into other cells still darker and more loathsome, shaped like a close jar, into which criminals were once lowered through the one opening at the top, but which now were entered by narrow doors.

The sides of these vaults were dripping with moisture, dull brown stalactites hung from the ceilings; the air was so foul we held our breath. The wretched inmates crowded around us offering wares made from the shells of cocoanuts, often carved with much skill. Their faces were brutal, their black hair was long and matted; their prison clothing was unclean, and as we passed by they cried out in mournful tones, "Pity us, senoritas! pity us, senoritas!" We were greatly moved at their sad fate and forgot their crimes, but the captain smiled and informed us that they were criminals of the very worst type and that one of the men was under condemnation for murdering and eating his own children.

Alas! they who had shown no mercy to others craved pity for themselves.

To this fortress and to the fatal swamps of Yucatan, the government sends these miserable offenders, where the yellow fever soon does the executioner's fatal work and spares the hangman's rope. No record is given of the termination of their wretched lives; the doors of the prison close against them and the world knows them no more. We bought some of their wares, and gladly hastened from the depressing scene. I said to Mr. Powell, upon re-entering the boat, "Ah, if we had known what was before us we should utterly have refused to land."

"Of course you would," he replied pleasantly, "that is the reason I did not inform you. It would never answer for you to leave Vera Cruz without seeing the prison of San Luis. You will not regret this experience."

Our bark sped gaily over the blue water, while the commander explained the powerful enginery on the wharves used for the lading and unlading of ships. We landed and examined the hulls of vessels attacked by the terrido, a destructive worm that infests the waters of the gulf and disables the stoutest ships. Nothing but copper sheathing can resist its tiny but relentless jaws.

We went back to our car in the broiling sun; we had no thermometer, but felt sure the register would be well up in the 90's, and this on the 4th day of

March. At ten a. m. we took leave of our kind host and were soon on our way back to the City of Mexico, glad to emerge from the Tierras Calientes.

We had for dinner this day a fish called pompano, found in thirty fathoms of water, the flesh of which, white and tender, is justly esteemed a great delicacy.

We reached Orizabe at eight p. m., and remained over night. M. Shirley, superintendent of the railroad, again met us and offered his aid. We are indebted to the officers of this road and of the Mexican Central for many favors which we shall not soon forget.

The next morning, March 5th, while we were at breakfast, the peon (who had done the braking for our car the day previous, and to whom the young ladies gave a trifle of money), came rushing across the track dressed in his Sunday suit of blue, gay sombrero and dashy red neckerchief. His face was wreathed in smiles, his hands were filled with bouquets. He sprang upon the steps of the car, the door was opened; with a graceful bow he presented the flowers and retired. The Mexican peon is nothing if not polite.

The day was uncomfortably warm, though cool winds from the home of perpetual snow moderated the heat. We strolled through the streets of Orizabe which is in order, cleanliness and thrift, superior to any other Mexican city it had been our fortune to visit. Glimpses through the grated windows disclosed pretty sitting-rooms and bed-chambers, neat and comfortable furniture, halls and courts full of flowers, gardens rank with banana and coffee trees, and shrubs with enormous tubular white blossoms, the name of which we did not learn.

In one of the gardens a school of children were seated under the trees repeating aloud their lessons in concert—a very pretty arcadian scene. We visited the market, returning through the shady Alameda, and after a walk of several miles, reached the cars at ten a. m., the hour fixed for our departure.

Again we climbed tremendous heights, swung upon a wire of steel over awful abysses, looked up to snow-capped mountains and down into dark ravines. Here, in the unremembered past, the forces of nature contended for mastery. Oh, the groaning, hissing, heaving, thundering, roaring that racked the elements, before Form and Silence subdued the struggling giants Fire and Water. And what has been, will be. What tremendous changes must yet be wrought upon the earth. What tides of humanity drifting around the globe; families, tribes, nations, races, willing or unwilling, driven, like autumn leaves before the gale, until the grand cycle is completed and the great cosmic night shall fall!

We reached the City of Mexico at eight p. m., and the next day made our final shopping tour, called upon our friends, and received a pressing invitation from our accomplished American minister, General Jackson, to remain for a grand dinner—an honor which we were compelled to decline.

Sunday, March 7th, was our last day in the city. We went to the Cathedral in the morning. This immense edifice is five hundred feet long and four hundred and twenty feet broad; so large that several priests, in different parts of the building, were saying mass at the same time. Here were to be seen thousands of kneeling worshippers. All classes were represented: abject peon mothers with babies in their arms; hideous Indians in tatters; poor deformed wretches, elegantly dressed senors and senoras, all kneeling indiscriminately upon the stone floor; some with eyes devoutly closed, some staring at each other or at the strangers.

The sight of this motley crowd, so abject, so reverent, so immoral, moved me greatly. Everybody tells the same sad story: their religion is worn upon the sleeve, it affects not their life, which is blackened by deceit, dishonesty and sensuality. To church in the morning, to the bull fight in the afternoon; in fact, Sunday is the only time when the brutal exhibition can be witnessed; to the pawnbrokers on Monday with the pelf gotten on Sunday.

The bull ring is about seven miles from the city, and it is painful to a humane soul to witness the departure of railroad trains loaded with men and women of high caste and low, that desecrate each Sabbath day and their own higher nature, by rushing to this place of infernal recreation. The bull fight is an outgrowth of Spanish ferocity, the original idea of which presupposed skill and courage in the picadors and matadors, but I am informed that the *sport* has degenerated into the slow butchery of five or six tortured bulls and horses, screens being placed for the ready protection of the men. Occasionally, however, a bull gets the advantage, and if a man or a horse is tossed and ripped up, the delighted spectators rend the air with cries of "Bravo! Good for the bull! Good for the bull!"

What can be expected of a people whose hours of Sabbath relaxation are spent amid such brutalizing atrocities? Alas, through what awful struggles must these souls pass if they ever attain to the kingdom of heaven!

After church we walked to the Alameda or public park, to listen to a *sacred concert*. Three bands were distributed through the ample groves, who dispensed music of the lightest, gayest character.

In the evening our friends called to bid us farewell; we part from them with regret, appreciating their great kindness, and hoping we may in some way be able to return it.

Chapter Seven.

FAREWELL TO MEXICO.

ITS CLIMATE AND PEOPLE—THE RETURN JOURNEY—CANYADA DISHONESTY—AT SILAO—NEW MEXICO—DESERTS AND DANGERS—INDIANS—A SAND STORM.

ALTHOUGH Mexico borders upon our own land, it is comparatively *terra incognita*, and in many respects more interesting to the traveler than Europe. The republic consists of twenty-seven states, one territory, and one district. It has thirty-five large cities, a population of nine millions, and an area of seven hundred and sixty-two square miles. It boasts every variety of climate and production, and, with the exception of the state of Vera Cruz, it is salubrious and delightful; the weather never interferes with out-door labor. The mining resources of Mexico are inexhaustible; with irrigation and proper mechanical appliances, the agricultural and horticultural possibilities are incalculable.

Though the atmosphere is dry and the few rivers anything but a blessing, Mexico is supplied with several wonderful springs which burst from the mountain sides in a manner little short of miraculous. There is one of these marvels of nature on the Vera

Cruz railroad, that disclosed itself when a rock was blasted during the construction. That at Augua Calientes is of hot water. The water of Lake Texcoco is salt, but the City of Mexico is bountifully supplied with pure, clear spring water from the heights of Chapultepec. We saw this astonishing stream rush into the reservoir like a river, from whence it is carried to the city in great conduits. It rises to the desired height by its own pressure, and is not affected by drought or rainfall.

The floating gardens in Lake Texcoco we did not visit for want of time. Their ancient splendor has departed. In fact, they are no longer floating, nor are they now gardens, except for culinary vegetables and fruits. Nevertheless they are thronged with a native population who preserve the ancient methods more perfectly on these fertile islands than in the city, and are consequently objects of great interest.

The dress, habits, dwellings and many of the manufactures suggest Italy, Syria and the Semetic tribes. In describing the peasant woman a writer remarks: "She is the representative of a race whose civilization is cöeval with the palmiest days of Egypt and Persia. Like her sister on the Ganges, the Nile and the Euphrates, she makes tortillas, or unleavened bread; she carries water on her head as gracefully as Rebecca, and spins like Penelope."

While our English ancestors were barbarians, living in mud huts, clad in the skins of wild beasts, there existed in Central America a mighty and highly civilized nation, of which the Mexican peon and his curious manufactures are now but a fast-fading reminiscence; for, with such a magnificent country, and every natural advantage unchanged, and a railroad one thousand two hundred and twenty-four miles long through the centre of the state, built by American enterprise at a cost of sixty millions of dollars, the nation now shows marks of decay and dissolution. The masses are superstitious, immoral and cruel; this last characteristic is an inevitable sequence of the others; they are dull and deficient in nerve-power; deformed, maimed and crippled persons abound; there is no enterprise, no element of progress. When urged to labor or action, the universal answer is, "To-morrow."

The government is faithless, unstable, always on the verge of revolution.

In leaving this beautiful country, so favored by nature, so cursed by man, many questions force themselves upon the mind of the philosopher and philanthropist. What causes have operated to produce its tribal and social conditions, so similar in many respects to that of Italy and the Orient? Are they the effect of an arid and equable climate? Are they due to the laws of heredity? How far are the individuals who compose that mixed population responsible? What will be the future of the state and government? What will become of the souls of these teeming millions?

Who can answer these questions? Who can fathom the mystery of the universe, the mystery of human existence?

Not one, save He who governs all.
"He knows, He knows."

Monday morning at eight o'clock we began our northward journey. The same bright sun, singing birds and shimmering trees that bade us welcome, now bestowed a farewell blessing.

The journey from Silao to Mexico, on our way down, was performed in the night. On our return we passed over that portion of the route by daylight. The luxuriance of the wonderful valley of Cañada was an astonishment and a delight. This remarkable tract of land lies between two ranges of lofty mountains, itself at an altitude of five thousand feet. It is only a few miles long, and is very narrow, yet here can be produced every variety of fruit and vegetable known to man. It is a bower, a jungle, an Eden of richest verdure.

The estates of the Mexican grandees are immense; one belonging to Terrassa is eighty-two miles in length, and in width "extends from horizon to horizon."

There are three crops of wheat in a year. Of many productions it may be said spring time and harvest are one. At Irapuato strawberries are always in season.

We learned that a robbery was perpetrated near Silao on March 2d. A party of mountain brigands derailed a freight train, stole the contents of the cars and escaped. They were pursued, captured, and fourteen of them summarily shot.

We had a personal experience on a small scale, of Mexican methods near the same place. One of our party bought a quantity of fruit while waiting at the station. She stood on the step of the car and placed the fruit beside her. The boy took the money, but returned only a part of the change which was due. The purchaser held out her hand showing the deficiency and exclaiming, "This is not enough!" At that moment the car began to move on, and the wretch of a boy, taking advantage of the situation, snatched the change out of her hand and at the same time swept the fruit off the step on to the ground, leaving the astonished purchaser minus fruit and money, plus a heavy load of vexation and chagrin. The increasing motion of the train made redress impossible, but the conductor said that he would see that the boy was punished, as there was no lack of witnesses to this bold larceny.

We remained over night at Silao, and as some of our party were desirous of procuring a specialty of the place, a gentleman who resided there offered to escort them to the shops. After their return, other gentlemen who were calling upon us in our car, expressed surprise that we should have allowed any of our party to go out unarmed. The young ladies replied quite nonchalantly, "Oh, Mr. Burton had his revolver!" I believe all the railroad officials carry weapons.

This same evening was very warm, and as we sat with the door of our car open, a crowd of beggarly creatures surrounded it, staring in at the doors and peering in through the windows. Presently four lusty Mexicans, armed to the teeth without, and primed by whiskey within, came upon the platform and saluting, asked permission to enter. Assent was given; they made the tour of the car, and with the usual " *Mil gracias,*" retired.

March 9th we continued our journey, always rumbling along over vast plains, hemmed in by lofty mountains. So perpetually are these features of landscape reproduced, we wonder if we are not the victims of illusion or enchantment, forever moving through a panorama that moves with us, or constantly reproduces itself.

About six o'clock p. m. we again passed the height of land near Zacatecas, which lies like a celestial city among silver hills at the stupendous altitude of eight thousand and forty-four feet, the home of seventy-five thousand souls. The mules are still climbing the mountains for ore, still turning the clumsy mills and treading out the harsh mud mixed with vitrol and mercury, and when the effect of the deadly chemicals have rendered them no longer fit for service, they are taken out and mercilessly shot. Ah! many changes must be wrought in human economy before this world will become a second Paradise!

After leaving Lerdo, the great cotton mart of Mexico, the verdure disappears, our course is over gray, sandy plains, producing only bunch grass and musquit bushes. Still, as the train goes on, the mountains pursue and hem us in. We reach El Paso after three days and two nights of travel.

Seventeen days have passed since we left El Paso on our outward trip; during this time we have traveled three thousand miles. How little we realize, by

the firesides of our homes, the immensity of these
distant lands, delineated on our maps by less than a
hand-breadth! We find letters from home, one of
which reads like fiction: "March 2d. ·For six mortal days a northwest blizzard has raged—the longest,
coldest, fiercest storm on record. Yesterday the
thermometer registered thirty degrees below zero;
the wind blew a hurricane. In the gusts, houses,
fences and barns would disappear; the house would
shake as if about to be crushed in. The water-pipes
have burst in every direction; we are in danger of a
water famine. With a raging fire in the furnace I
cannot sleep for the cold."

During these days we were in the Tierras Calientes,
amidst tropical heat and verdure.

A dull, eventless, objectless ride takes us to Albuquerque in New Mexico, through a monotony of gray
plains and distant mountains. The sluggish, muddy
Rio Grande struggles through the flat sands, picking
its way along the shallow depressions, sometimes
stopping to dream; no—pausing from very vacuity of
thought, forgetting its fluvial destiny and degenerating into a muddy pool.

How unlike our dashing, energetic, crystal streams,
turning wheels, buoying boats, coquetting with flowery banks, laughing at the trees whose outstretched
arms vainly implore them to linger.

Poor, dull Rio Grande! Neither business nor pleasure await thy tardy footsteps. No puffing steamer
with trumpeting engine, no noisy mill with clamorous wheel, no gay launch with music and laughter,

rouse thy drowsy energies or demand thine elemental aid. No waving shrub beckons, no bright-eyed flower nods a mock caress. A dreary, joyless, pulseless life is thine, save when the overburdened skies pour out their torrent of tears, and thou, in blind, unreasoning sympathy, dost rise and swell in fury, carrying destruction and desolation along thy path.

March 12th we took breakfast in our car at a place called Luna—rightly named, for it is naught but moonshine. Not a solitary building, not even a shanty, marks the city's centre or circumference. A small board or shingle upholds the name and honor of this empty place. I called the attention of the conductor to the exceeding smallness of the city of Luna. He acknowledged the fact and added: "There are about fifty miles to a man in this part of New Mexico." But then, it would take about fifty miles of sand, wind and muddy water to support one man.

In this territory is the Navajaho Indian reservation. There seems little to live upon, but fortunately there are few people to live. Our steward went into a restaurant on the line of the railroad, where supper is provided for passengers, and inquired for milk. "Milk!" was the indignant reply; "I haven't seen a drop for three days. How can you expect milk where there are neither cows, goats, or even *asses?*" A horrible suspicion crosses our mind—the milk we have been drinking never came from a Jersey cow!

At midnight we passed over the Cañon Diabolo, an awful fissure in the mountains, five hundred and forty feet in width. Across this yawning gulf an iron trestle bridge is suspended: above it towers a lofty mountain, over which, at this solemn hour, the young moon peered curiously, but was powerless to penetrate the black shadows in its depths. Two days ago, as a freight train was passing near this place, a boulder became loosened from the height above, rolled down, struck the engine and hurled it into the gulf below. The engineer saved himself by jumping, but the fireman was killed and the brakeman badly injured. Railroading in the wilds of nature is no trifling affair, necessitating, as it does, horse-shoe and reversed curves, along almost inaccessible ledges, hair-hung bridges across volcanic gulfs, and embankments through the beds of treacherous streams. In the construction of some portions of these, as of the Mexican roads, men worked on the sheer precipice with ropes round their bodies fastened to the trunks of trees, the debris being carried away in blankets on the backs of men.

At the stations in New Mexico and Arizona are to be seen straggling groups of nomad Indians of different tribes, always ill-formed, dark creatures, with coarse faces and black hair, generally hanging down their shoulders. Most of the men wore blankets, but we saw some young bucks with only a cloth around the loins. We noticed that many of the Mojaves were painted in black, blue and red stripes or patches, and have since learned by the public prints, that they are now on the war path, although our government provides for their support. We saw one young buck of the Hualapai tribe on horse back, lazily trotting along the prairie, while his squaw ran in front carrying the baby, a spectacle that called out some spicy comments from the young ladies of our party.

The eastern slope of the divide in this part of the continent shows unmistakable evidence of the reign of fire; on the west are indications of the domain of Old Ocean. "Here," says a recent observer, "many miles from either fresh or salt water, may be found the beach of an ancient ocean, and, thickly scattered on hill and dale, once unmistakably forming the bottom of the forgotten sea, are found immense whalebones, millions of shells of all varieties and great masses of coral, all telling more plainly than written book the tale of some gigantic convulsion of nature that has driven the waters back to their present bounds, and left a dismal waste where once undoubtedly the ships of mariners in the long ago were wont to float." We crossed the great Mojave Desert. So barren, desolate and vast is it that the whistle and rush of the threadlike train, waking echoes that have slumbered for milleniums, seem a rash desecration. Trackless plains of sand stretch away in every direction to the foot of purple or indigo mountains, sometimes naught but sand or clay, and sometimes scraggy with a stunted growth of nameless gray weeds, whose scowling aspect seems a protest against the fate that compels them to germinate in such a desolate waste.

Toward night a sand storm came on. The conductor hurried in and warned us to close doors and windows. The distant landscape disappeared, a gray cloud swallowed up the scene, the wind threatened to be dangerous, but only a wing of the storm crossed our track. Yet the meterological disturbance continued, and the conductor lay by on a shelf of the mountain nearly two hours in the night, fearing the train would be blown off the track; a wise precaution, for even then the cars swayed so that we were almost thrown from our berths.

Chapter Eight.

LOS ANGELES.

THE CITRUS LAND—SAN MONICA—THE THIRTY MILE DRIVE — PASADENA — MADRE VILLA — THE ROUTE TO SAN FRANCISCO — PERILOUS RAILROADING.

MARCH 15th we reached Los Angeles, having traveled, since we left home, nearly seven thousand miles by rail; from the Poles to the Tropics, and *vice versa* many times, judging by the thermometer. March 13th we woke in the midst of a young winter. Snow covered the ground, water pipes were frozen, icicles hung upon the engine tender. Now, March 15th, our eyes were greeted with vineyards and groves, green meadows and pastures, where cattle and horses stood knee-deep in the grass; thrifty looking farm buildings, cloud-capped mountains and moist blue skies fill up the scene. We were glad to rest at a hotel after twelve days and nights confinement to our car.

As we stopped at the station a man, who was unshackling the car, mused thus: "Bellevue, Central Vermont. This must be a Boston party, but *I don't see the beans!*"

People on the other side of the continent have as little idea of our geography as we have of theirs, and it was rather mortifying, when asked where we were from, to be obliged to explain in our reply, "From Vermont, *near Boston.*"

Mystery of sunlight and moisture, the Citrus garden of America! The earth is a carpet of living green, the patterns wrought in flowers. In our approach to the city we passed through a forest of orange trees, twelve miles in length. Here are single groves of thirty thousand trees—not only of oranges, but lemons, limes and grape-fruit. The redundant evergreen foilage, dark and glossy, contrasts beautifully with the golden fruit and snow-white blossoms seen upon the trees at the same time. It is often difficult to determine which of the three colors prevails, while cords of the fruit lie upon the ground. English walnuts, olives, grapes and raisins are also cultivated for exportation.

Shade trees grow luxuriantly. The cypress, a very delicate cedar, the pepper tree, (a glorified mountain ash) with long sprays of red berries, the eucalyptus (the blue gum tree of Australia), and every variety of pine are principally used, and are all evergreen. Birds live in their branches; among these are flocks of the sweet-voiced, clamorous linnet. Flowers cover wall, terrace and lawn; geraniums attain the dignity of hedges eight feet high; heliotropes become bushes, calla lilies are used as borders, vines open their bright blossoms on the very tops of tall trees, as if striving to catch the first caress of the cool, crisp breezes descending from the snow-clad Sierra Madre.

Los Angeles, situated near the Pacific coast, on the

thirty-fourth degree of latitude, is a city of thirty thousand inhabitants. The varied character of the population is manifest in the mixture of northern enterprise and southern thriftlessness. The soil is a rich black loam, and the climate, as upon the western coast of all continents, is more genial and equable than upon the eastern. This may be due to the rotary motion of the earth, which causes the eastern shores to catch the first violence of the grand atmospheric draught, leaving the western coasts protected, as it were, under the lee of the land; or it may be the modifying influence of those great water currents, the Mexican and Japanese Gulf Streams; or there may be magnetic causes beyond the reach of human speculation. Be this as it may, the Pacific slope is warmer than the Atlantic; though, from local causes, storms and other atmospheric convulsions are more violent. In January last a cloud burst in the Sierra Madre mountains, and following the river's course, flooded the lower portion of the city of Los Angeles, carrying away twenty-five houses, a part of the bridge and all of the tramway in its path. Wonderful to relate, only two lives were lost, as the cataclysm occurred in the daytime, and people were warned by the awful roar. Let New Englanders be thankful, that if their climate is less equable, the storms are more so. And in this connection I would observe that the average of health at Los Angeles seems no greater than ours; lung disease and malaria prevail; we were more nearly ill at this place than at any other during our absence.

Tuesday morning, March 16, we ran down by railway to Santa Monica, the port of Los Angeles, eighteen miles distant. The hotel looked so ill-kept and unattractive we went directly to the shore and had our first view of the Pacific Ocean; we saw it afterward under far different auspices. On this day it was dull, the watery plain was gray and illimitable, rolling in vast surges, its heavy heart forever palpitating against the shore. Perhaps the fatigue of the long journey affected our spirits, or the dull shadows on sea and land, portents of a coming storm, gave sombre coloring to our thought. The ocean's solemn moan told of dreadful secrets in its sunless crypts; of battered hulks, of stained and draggled pennons, misshapen figure heads, and limp, decaying sails; of unused, forgotten treasure, riches heaped up and none to gather; of the shriek "of some strong swimmer in his agony," the gurgling sob of despair, the still, pale face and sightless eyes upturned to the far off, yellow sun; of little fishes scared by the waving robes; of cruel monsters that seize their unresisting prey. The sea, hoary with grief and age, the helpless cause and witness of all this woe, can only sigh and moan.

We sat and dreamed upon the cliff for hours, then wandered beneath the eucalyptus trees, forgot poetry and lowered our dignity sufficiently to partake of peanuts and oranges, and at three p. m. returned by train to Los Angeles.

The next day we took the celebrated Horse Shoe Drive of thirty miles. The route is through the town of Pasadena (the Pass of Eden), where, on a lofty height, Mr. Raymond, of the Passumpsic railroad, is building an elegant hotel; thence to the Sierra Madre Villa, a charming retreat embowered in orange groves, under the shadow of the dark Madre mountains, through the plantation of Mr. Rose, returning by the Mission and wine manufactory of San Gabriel. The scenery on this drive is said to be the finest in the country, and of its type no doubt this is true; but the equinoctial storm, which was brooding over the sea on the day previous, broke in fury while we were out, and we saw these beauties through a mist of nature's tears. As we drew near Los Angeles, on our return, we passed through a valley surrounded by treeless but verdant hills, all of brightest coloring; on the vast plain thousands of sheep were feeding. A shepherd stood near them with a dog and a wolfish animal, that the driver told us was a domesticated coyote.

The equinoctial storm wrought so much damage to the railroads we were obliged to remain at Los Angeles longer than we desired. The hotel is untidy, the table and service wretched, the prices extravagant, the air insalubrious, and, Monday, March 22d, we gladly took our departure for San Francisco.

Our route lay between lofty mountains, no longer barren, but clad with verdure to the very tops; the fields at their feet were flower gardens.

We went through a tunnel seven thousand feet long on a continuous up-grade the entire distance. We made the passage in utter darkness, having neglected to light our lamps. The way seemed interminable, as if we were bound for the lower regions, a feeling not lessened by the fact that an accident, the caving in of the tunnel, had occurred only two days before.

The heavy rain of the last week had washed the road, and the Los Angeles River had flooded the valley. It is a very disagreeable peculiarity of these rivers, that when water is greatly needed their broad beds are dry sand and stone; and in the rainy season, when they would be better dry, they rise to mad, destructive torrents. Upon this occasion, as upon many previous, the works of puny man were swept away. Hastily constructed tracks and embankments were thrown up as soon as the flood subsided, and over these rickety, unsubstantial works our tottering train, " like a wounded serpent dragged its huge length along." Our engine, a monster of one hundred and five tons, gave token by its laborious breathing of another mountain ascent, this time over the Tehatchpi range. A fearful expedient was adopted to obtain the indispensable grade. The track makes what is called a loop. It passes *over* a tunnel, down a steep in a helicoid, or screw spiral, which runs round and returns to the same point low enough to pass *through* the tunnel it just before surmounted. I hope I may never take another such ride; we seemed to hang upon the ragged edge of nothingness. There are many stretches of embankment now abandoned, where attempts have been made to meet the caprice of the stream in vain. All honor to the men who struggle thus patiently with the blind forces of nature.

Night overtakes us on this dangerous journey; we retire to rest, but sleep is broken. We miss the smooth rumble that acts as a lullaby; the car rocks like a storm-vexed ship; a sense of danger mingles with the momentary dreams, in which tired nature tries to assert her rights. Morning dawns; we rise unrefreshed, but thankful that we live to rise at all. At the town of Modesta we are still one hundred and twenty-seven miles from San Francisco, three hours late.

Chapter Nine.

MONTEREY.

OAKLAND — STUPENDOUS ADVERTISEMENTS — HOTEL DEL MONTE — CASTLES IN SPAIN — BATHS — THE SEVENTEEN MILE DRIVE.

"Angels fold their wings and rest
In this Eden of the West."

WE reached Oakland, the railroad terminus, at twelve m., and went into the reception room of the depot to await the ferry-boat that conveys passengers across an arm of the bay into the city of San Francisco. The room is arranged like a chapel, with a platform at one end and numerous seats fronting it; but the enormous, gaudy advertisements that adorn the walls dispel any possible illusion that this is a sacred edifice. On one side the goddess of love and a family of cupids, life-size and highly colored, are seated on the banks of a lily-pond, and are supposed to be calling public attention to a Domestic sewing machine.

Beside this practical hint to family affection and duty, is the picture of a man on horseback, large as life, fierce as a Mexican freebooter, tearing through a vast desert, waving aloft, not a revolver, but a bottle marked Mineral Water.

Near by this startling design, Columbia, Goddess of Liberty, with several questionable looking associates, one a female Mercury (at least she had wings on her head), is majestically pointing to a shoe store. In another place, a man and woman in gay attire, attitudinizing as if for photographs, sit at a table loaded with eatables, to prefigure the delights of a restaurant. This colossal group, in drawing and expression, caps the climax of fine art.

On the opposite side of the room is a bottle of champagne at least six feet tall; the cork is blown out of sight and a column of froth goes up from the neck like the smoke of a volcano, true indication, no doubt, of the elevating effects of the wine proclaimed beneath in enormous red letters. Near this bold defiance of the temperance cause is a companion piece. Madame Adelina Patti, gigantic in size, stands with a sheet of music in hand, chanting in doggerel rhyme the praises of a cigarette. This picture was, I think, six feet square. The song ran as follows:

> "What a pleasure of an evening,
>   When your day's work is done,
> To take your Patti Cigarettes
>   And smoke them one by one;
> And as you watch the clouds arise,
>   And gaily puff away,
> You light another cheerfully,
>   And then you're bound to say:
> 'Patti, Patti, that's the name!'
>   And like that great artiste,
> Well known to fame,
>   As soon as you've smoked one
> You'll like them, you bet,
>   You're bound to enjoy
> The Patti Cigarette!

The poet forgot to mention the opium, arsenic and other deadly narcotics that compose this enchanting compound.

These are but specimens of the dashing topics that tapestry the walls. In the concoction of stupendous advertisements California defies the world.

While we were gazing awe-struck at these astonishing devices, the great ferry-boat steamed in, but no place for the egress of anxious passengers was visible.

Presto! Up goes an immense land advertisement at the end of the hall. An ocean, a range of mountains and a prairie disappear, and in their place, lo! a broad walk leading most conveniently to the deck of the steamer.

There we ran the gauntlet of hack-drivers, clamoring like frogs in a dry time. One burly, well-conditioned fellow, worthy of being an alderman, at least in physical qualifications, outdid Sam Weller in confidential manner. He was evidently "laying for us." (I drop into slang, adopting my style to the subject.) With numerous winks and nods he said: "I know where you want to go—Jones, of the Palace, sent me to look out for your party. He's pretty well filled up, but he's all heeled for you." With this somewhat problematical assurance we crossed the ferry with our confidential guide, who put us into a carriage and drove through crowded streets to the hotel.

One of our party had contracted a stubborn cold at Los Angeles, and it was deemed advisable to try a change of air. We therefore hastened our departure for the sanitarium of California, Monterey, an old Spanish town on the coast, one hundred and twenty miles nearly south of San Francisco. Our journey was through a fertile country, much like New England in the leafy month of June.

It was quite dark, without moon or star, when we arrived at the station of the Hotel Del Monte. Nothing was visible but a crowd of passengers hurrying to a lamp-lit omnibus that looked in the dim perspective longer and narrower than a railroad car. Into this vehicle I desperately struggled, for danger and wreck seemed imminent in such an ill-constructed carriage and Cimerean driveway; but I said Kismet, and resigned myself to the inevitable. The timbers creak, the wheels rotate, the gravel crunches, the ponderous vehicle, with two opposite ranks of human beings, armed with umbrellas and barricaded behind traveling satchels, yields to unseen forces; it is propelled forward and upward; it rumbles through black night; it stops, we pitch forward, hospitable hands receive us, we are ushered into a large, brilliantly lighted hall. A fire of logs is blazing on an ample hearth, a hundred guests in groups enjoy its genial influence and watch the arrival of new comers. The voice of the landlord announces that our rooms on the first floor are ready, and dinner awaits us. We dine and retire, close our eyes to the dense outer darkness and sleep the sleep of the just—when the just are fatigued by a long journey and rest by the shores of the sounding sea.

March 30th we open our eyes on the full-fledged day. Are we still dreaming? Nay, this is startling, amazing reality—we have found our Castles in Spain! From the long, low windows of our parlor, through the vine-clad arches of a broad veranda, are seen green lawns sloping away to a lake, from the middle of which rises a cloud-like fountain climbing to the skies: in the mist rainbows play, and on the shore Swiss cottages nestle. Shadows of ancient oaks and giant evergreens lie upon the grass where innumerable flowers disdain not to bloom. Birds sing in the branches, dark men in foreign attire dress the lawn and sprinkle the plants. Our surprise and delight is greater than that of the Grand Monarch of France when he awoke in his palace at Versailles and caught the gleam of the Swiss lake, the magic result of one night's toil.

Yes, we have found our Castles in Spain, the Spanish name, Del Monte, assures us; and more than this, we have taken possession.

We perform a careful toilet as becomes Spanish proprietors. We go out into the ancestral halls; the floors are covered with carpets; fires are burning on the hearths, for mornings in this lordly mansion are cool. The broad halls, the tall columns and vaulted domes overpower us, but it is with delight, and when the demand of grosser nature calls to the banquet room, the golden apples of the Hesperides crown the board, but no Discordia placed them there.

Our repast is over, and we go forth among the guests. They take slight notice of our coming; indeed, there is a look in some of their faces as if they, too, are Spanish proprietors. This gives us a strange feeling. Is it possible that our claim "is only such stuff as dreams are made of?"

We walk through the extensive grounds, observe the growth of tree and vine, admire the tall heliotrope hedges and the white roses that climb to the eaves of the lofty portico; we wonder at the curious forms the live oaks have attained, we commend the taste our servants have displayed in the arrangement of flower beds, walks and drives. We wander to the shore and listen with rapture to the slow, infrequent pulsations of the sea—the water is calm, nor wind nor tide vex its surface, but an occasional long-drawn sigh heaves its mighty breast.

"There's a sound in the deep
Like the murmuring breath of a lion asleep."

Our joy is full. What though the "children of Alice call Bertram father?" Do not our own walk beside us, enjoying as we do, our Castles in Spain?

Here we spend the last days of March, the stormy month. The sky is bright, the birds carol in the tall trees, the guests stroll through the groves, bask in the sunshine or drive in carriages. The grounds of this magnificent hotel are seven thousand acres in extent, and boast twenty-seven miles of driveway—fifty men are employed in their care; the head gardener is German, the assistants are Chinese. Here reigns perpetual spring—May in January, June in March. Plants of tropic deltas grow near the gray, uncouth forms of a northern desert. The Arizona garden "shows every variety of outline seen in the diabolical cactus, fascinating by its repulsiveness," and astonishing by gorgeous blossoms that seem to alight upon the prickly spines, like birds or butterflies.

We explore the Labyrinth. This production of man's ingenuity is formed of cypress hedges so skilfully arranged that one may walk for miles without finding the centre, and once inside miles may intervene between it and the place of egress. It is a source of great amusement, for, after energetically pursuing a long course, one is stopped by a blank wall, and patiently retracing his steps finds himself perhaps in the same cul-de-sac. The hedge is higher than the tallest man, and it gave a strange sensation to catch glimpses of other bewildered travelers running back and forth, laughing and shouting to each other and to us, so near that our hands could have clasped through the hedge while we were perhaps a mile distant by the path. After many ludicrous mistakes we penetrated the innermost fold of this leafy labyrinth, and almost expected to find within it a devouring dragon and an enchanted princess; but the illusion was dispelled by the sight of some very common benches placed there to await the tired pedestrian. One poor lady got lost in the maze and became panic-stricken, but her cries and screams brought help from the laborers in that part of the ground.

A Herdic runs once an hour to and from the baths and the town of Monterey. It is a strange vehicle, painted red, half omnibus and half wagonette. The coachman is a little old hunchback, with puffy cheeks and head sunken between his shoulders. He never speaks, and I never saw him off the seat of the Herdic. I do not know if he can speak or walk; he rings a bell as the carriage starts.

As this uncanny equipage stands waiting at or drives from the door, one rubs his eyes and opens them wide to test the accuracy of his vision; he feels as if he had been set back to the medieval times when dwarfs and mutes played an important part in the household of their lords. However, it took us safely through the shady road, and, without a word from the dwarf, drew up in front of the bath house. We alighted, and after passing along the platform and through an entry, were ushered into a spacious hall lighted by a glass roof. Here were four large tanks of sea-water, separated by decks and supplied with stairways that lead into the tanks; also slides about fifteen feet high, from which swimmers can plunge into the water. Around the hall tropical plants were growing, which, with the great swimming tanks, gave an effect of oriental luxury. The water is heated by steam, and at this hour was full of bathers in costume, diving, plunging, swimming and floating. A beautiful child about five years old, a daughter of Mr. Seward, of New York, stood on the deck waiting for her father. Presently he took her in his arms and went into the water; sometimes carrying her on his shoulder or swimming with her on his back; sometimes he placed his hands under her chest to steady her, and the little creature paddled with hands and feet like a water sprite. It was a very pretty and unusual sight, reminding one of the legend of Saint Christopher and the infant Jesus. A crowd of spectators witnessed the scene and an artist photographed it. Subsequently our own party patronized the baths and found the recreation delightful.

These baths are pronounced the finest in America, and perhaps in the world; they are situated on a smooth beach, which we visited after leaving the buildings. The water of the Pacific is not gray like that of our ocean, it is of a beautiful greenish blue; the roll also seems longer. Everything in this part of the world is upon the grandest scale.

In the afternoon we go out into the grounds, walk in the shade of the great trees and rest upon the seats which everywhere open their hospitable arms. Not a breath of air or a leaf is stirring; the lofty evergreens, in dignified silence, uprear themselves against the silent sky; no sound of bird or insect disturbs the still repose. The effect is like enchantment; we forget time and grief and care, our former life, our distant home—even the faces of our friends fade from the tablet of memory; the tranquility of nature permeates body and soul. Have we not eaten of the flowers of forgetfulness that grow in the valley of dreams? The shadows seem always pointing to the east. It is the Land of the Evening Calm!

Chapter Ten.

MONTEREY.

THE SEVENTEEN MILE DRIVE—PACIFIC GROVE—SEALS—CEDARS OF LEBANON—A LUDICROUS INCIDENT—THE LONE CYPRESS—A WONDERFUL SCENE—STORY OF A BANDIT.

MONDAY, April 5th, we took the celebrated drive through the company's land. An open carriage and a span of horses were secured for this purpose. The driver was a grave, quiet man from Canada, who bore the familiar name of Paul Smith, and whose eighteen years residence in California made him an excellent guide.

We drove through the town of Monterey, where we saw a cross bearing date 1770, the year that the Spaniards landed on these shores, also the old wooden building where the first legislature of California met in 1849, and the fortifications used by General Fremont during the Mexican war.

Near this place is a cluster of low sheds devoted to whaling purposes. Watchmen at Monterey are always on the lookout seaward, and when a fitful mist appears moving on the waves, indicating the presence of an adventurous whale in the bay, a vessel is immediately sent in pursuit, and if a capture is effected, the blubber is reduced to oil in these buildings. Great heaps of whitening bones bear witness to successful battles with these monsters of the deep.

A similar cluster of buildings, called Chinatown, marks the spot where large quantities of fish are taken and preserved by the busy foreigners. The fish on this coast are plentiful and fine. The pompano, cod, rockfish, Spanish mackerel, smelt and bonita are had in their season. The salmon, which come from the Colorado river, are the finest I have ever seen.

We made the tour of the Pacific Grove, a beautiful plot of land belonging to the Pacific Improvement Company, the same who own the Hotel del Monte. It is designed for camp-meetings, conventions, residences, etc. Many lovely little cottages are already built, similar to those at Martha's Vineyard. After leaving the Grove our course lay through a romantic road overshadowed by pine trees, and sweet with their wholesome perfume. It was also beautified by wild lilacs in full bloom, and numerous other flowering shrubs which flourish in this lonely spot, called by the Spaniards, "Lovers' Lane." Such lanes, however, are not peculiar to the Spaniards or to California. I have noticed their prevalence in all the countries I have visited, and I suppose they will continue to exist as long as men and women walk the earth together, but I must own that one is rarely seen so conducive to tender emotion as the aforesaid lane, winding through the dark forest that skirts the shore of the grandest ocean.

As we drove along beneath the aromatic pines,

caught glimpses of the blue waves, felt the rush of the wild winds and listened to the pulsating surge, we remembered the words of Byron :

> "There is a pleasure in the pathless woods,
> There is a rapture on the lonely shore,
> There is society where none intrudes
> By the deep sea, and music in its roar."

We came to a cove where shells and other marine treasures are often found driven in by wind and wave from distant islands, and left the carriage to try our fortune. The wind, which had been fresh from the time of our setting out, had now risen to a gale; it blew from the land, and strove with the incoming tide; the great palpitating plain was lashed into foam, the white caps contrasting with the tumultuous waves rendered them more "deeply, darkly, beautifully blue." The long surges rolled in with majestic sweep and were driven back, shattered like flying snow-drifts. As they surmounted a hidden reef off the shore, an effect was produced grand and almost terrible. For a moment a mighty commotion was evident under the sea, then two tremendous opposing waves, like great dragons, upreared their crests, dashed forward and grappled as in deadly fray. After a furious struggle, in which neither obtained the mastery, they sank exhausted to rally for another and another onset. The battlefield was limitless, the combatants were gigantic, the struggle interminable; and, fascinated by the wildness of the scene, we watched it from the bluff, unmindful of our peril, till the wind, ferocious as the wave, nearly swept us into the sea. Being reminded of the object of our coming, the coveted treasures of the deep, we glanced around to see if any were within reach; naught but broken fragments glittered among the rocks, and the footsteps of the ubiquitious Chinaman appeared in the sand; we therefore crept carefully down from our dangerous outlook, and subsequently procured the shells at second hand.

At this place one of our party met with a ludicrous mishap. His overcoat, which was left in the carriage while we climbed the rocks, was, on our return, no where to be found. Presuming it had been blown away by the violence of the wind, we turned the horses and carefully retraced our steps. Soon the missing garment was discovered tumbling its stupid way over the beach, apparently bent upon plunging into the deep. To avert such an ill-timed catastrophe, the alarmed owner sprung from the vehicle and gave the flying overcoat chase. But scarcely had he reached the ground before the mischievous gale seized his eye-glasses and hurled them away. In groping for them (he could not see without their aid), he lost his hat, and for a moment it seemed as if the tragedy of unfortunate Dr. Wango Tango was about to be re-enacted, but the party in the carriage went to the rescue, the suicidal overcoat was dragged from the brink of a watery grave, the recalcitrant hat and eye-glasses were captured and subdued, their possessor shook himself together again, serenity was restored, and we resumed our journey.

That ladies, under the circumstances, would become somewhat dismembered was to be expected, but that one of the sterner sex should go to pieces in such an incoherent manner, was a great surprise and a bewilderment.

Soon afterward we passed a group of jagged rocks which numerous seals occupy as a playground. The rocks were brown and the water was alive with these interesting animals.

Our way now took us through a very remarkable grove of ancient trees, utterly unlike any others we had seen, and unknown on the continent save in this one locality. They are apparently the veritable cedars of Lebanon. The grove is large, but the trees are old and rapidly becoming extinct; many are already naked skeletons, grotesque and ghastly spectres, bleached by wind and sun.

As our carriage was slowly making its way over a precipitous ledge the driver brought his horses to a stand, and pointing down the steep toward the sea he said, "There is the Lone Cypress." Upon a great rock, entirely bare of other vegetation, which had apparently been torn from the ledge and had fallen into the sea, stood one of the beautiful cedars of Lebanon in stately solitude. How came it in this lonely spot? Imagination was at once excited and piqued. Had it been banished from the presence of its peers in the forest above for some unpardonable offense? Or, had the evil passions of its comrades, fear and envy, doomed it, though innocent, to this rocky St. Helena? Or, was it a misanthrope, a hermit-tree, who, tired of the society of its fellows, disappointed in love, and defeated in ambition, had voluntarily left its native grove and sought this desolate crag to vegetate and die?

But the reverie was brief; our eyes were drawn on and beyond this strange foreground; exclamations of wonder burst from every lip. The vast ocean lay before us, its color vivid green or blue, hurrying white caps and long rolling waves beat the curved shore that bears the name Half-Moon. A high, bold promontory, called Mt. Carmel, walls off the land, and at the foot of the terminating headland a group of ragged, rocky islands project out of the foamy waves.

A great bank of fog was rising over the distant sea where land and water meet; a strange transparent haze or nimbus, betokening the advance of a storm. The precipitous ledge where we were standing, was covered with lofty trees, behind us were the skeleton cedars, beneath us the bald rock and the "Lonely Cypress;" and over all the bright sun was shining. The scene was indescribably beautiful, but that which enhanced its marvelous effect was what no picture can boast, no description convey—*sound* and *motion;* the tumult of the waves, the wild tossing of the trees, the roar of the wind, the thunder of the surge. Our garments fluttered in the gale; a long red shawl which I vainly strove to confine, broke from restraint and streamed away in gyrating folds, like a flying dragon; our ears were distracted by the noise; we were conscious of strange electric thrills; it were slight stretch of fancy to imagine a host of elemental spirits rushing around us.

We lingered; there was a hush in the blast, and the interest of this memorable hour was intensified and its colors made permanent by a story told us there.

A few years ago, the rocky islands, which we now saw lying in the mist below the mountains, were the haunt of a notorious Spanish bandit, by name Vasquez. For seven or eight years this desperado and his band were the terror of the Pacific coast. With infernal skill and success he planned and perpetrated the most cold-blooded robberies and murders. In the dark night he would swoop down on a lonely traveler or sleeping hamlet, carry away whatever he valued, and leave naught but death and desolation behind. He defied the law and its officers, for when pursued he would retreat with his banditti to the impregnable fortresses of his sea-encircled caverns.

But, by the fiat of nature's inexorable law, lives of violence must come to a violent end. "Whosoever sheddeth man's blood, by man shall his blood be shed."

A bounty was placed upon the head of Vasquez; he might be taken dead or alive. After many wonderful escapes, perhaps he grew careless, or allowed some overmastering passion to lull him into momentary forgetfulness. A resolute sheriff from Los Angeles surprised him and his gang at a place of rendezvous on the main land. After a desperate struggle, in which several of the outlaws were shot, Vasquez, who happened at the moment to be unarmed, was taken alive. He was carried to Sacramento, securely ironed, and there, at the age of thirty-five, suffered the penalty of his crimes upon the gallows.

After listening to this story and gazing once more upon the transcendent scene, made memorable by these adventures, we silently pursued our way.

A ride of five miles, past a deep canyon, brought us once more to the town of Monterey, where we called at the store of Dr. Heintz, who has in his possession a living horned toad. This specimen, seven or eight inches long, was gray, with the tail of a lizard; upon the back of his head was a flat shield-like appendage with serrated edges, out of which the bright eyes peered — no doubt the fabled "diamonds in the toad's head."

The wind increased to a furious gale before we reached the hotel, and the next morning the threatened storm broke over land and sea.

We cannot do justice to this ideal retreat in our limited space. The extensive grounds are beautified by gardens, bowers, bowling alleys, tennis, archery and croquet courts, sand-beds for children to play in, swings, baths, *et cetera*, all on the most liberal scale. Flowers are numerous and rare; one rose tree is eighteen or twenty feet high, with a stem one foot in circumference. We saw here for the first time a passion flower vine loaded with crimson blossoms. The buildings are commodious and in admirable proportion. The table is excellent; the service all that could be desired. The waiters are many of them grave and reverend men, giving the impression of retired clergymen or college professors in disguise.

The guests who congregate here to spend the winter months are people of wealth, refinement and principle, dignified and self-contained, but who know enough of the world to make the most and best of their accidental companionship; there is no emulation, no ultra fashionable element. The climate is equable, the thermometer ranging only from fifty-one to sixty-eight through the entire year; yet the nights are cold and we are warned not to trust the evening air. Great roaring fires are kept up in the public rooms and steam heaters modify the atmosphere in the remote halls. With all these advantages the prices are moderate—two and one-half dollars per day. Our visit of ten days was all too brief, but we could not linger forever.

> "Sitting all day in a silver mist,
> In silvery silence all the day,
> Save for the low, soft plash of spray
> And lisp of sands by water kissed,
> As the tide creeps up the bay.
>
> Little we hear and little we see,
> Wrapped in a veil by fairies spun,
> The solid earth is melting away,
> The shining hours pass noiselessly
> A woof of shadow and sun.
>
> But a storm that we felt not had risen and rolled
> While lost in this fair reverie,
> And when we awoke in the morning, behold,
> Our castle had vanished away."

Chapter Eleven.

SAN FRANCISCO.

THE CITY OF GOLD—CHINATOWN—WESTERN WEATHER.

WE left Monterey April 8th, and the same evening reached San Francisco, a city well known to all your readers, and which many of them have visited; description would be superfluous. Everybody has heard of the Palace Hotel, an edifice that merits the royal appellation, with one thousand and sixteen rooms, capable of accommodating two thousand eight hundred guests. They have seen the wondrous locomotion of cable cars, like Southey's Ship of Heaven:

> "Hands that we cannot see let slip
> The cable of that magic ship;
> Swift as an arrow in its flight
> The car shoots by in day or night,
> Smooth as a swan when not a breeze at even
> Disturbs the surface of the silver stream,
> Through storm or sunshine sails the Ship of Heaven."

How greatly differing from that of the poet laureate is the description of the Chinaman: "No pushee, no pullee; go like hellee!"

Your readers know all about the land-locked harbor, embosomed in hills, beautiful as a mountain lake; they have heard of the Seal Rocks, where the strange amphibia swim like fishes, climb like monkeys, play like puppies and roar like lions; they have visited the Mint, Chinatown, the Joss Houses and all the Golden Places—the Golden Gate, the Golden Park, the Golden Street (albeit not leading to the New Jerusalem); they have perchance made purchases at the store of the Golden Rule and have found a fleece unlike that of Greek fable: if fond of narcotics they may have smoked the Golden Clip; they may have walked in the Golden Way and lodged at the Golden Bee.

Friends call upon us: the talk is of gold, or its equivalent. One would suppose that King Midas had gone tipsy through the streets, reeling against everything as he passed; everything seems golden but the lining of our purses: strange to say, that rapidly degenerates into nickel-plate.

Everybody is wide awake; eyes are like hawks; motions quick and restless. The streets are mostly up hill and down; thoroughfares are thronged; the shops and goods are handsome, the prices high.

San Francisco is situated on sandy, treeless hills and rocks. It is irregular and uneven, reminds one of the Island of Jamaica, which is likened in its topography to a crumpled piece of paper. The streets are ill-paved, the buildings wanting in architectural beauty, though the more recent public structures and the dwellings of the millionaires are very fine.

But San Francisco is not yet fifty years old; its growth and prosperity, since the discovery of gold in

'49, is without precedent; its defects are merely those of youth.

Perhaps more than a passing notice should be given to Chinatown. Thither we were drawn, as by a magnet, and once in these strange quarters seemed to be in the celestial empire; and we were in reality nearer the coast of Japan than our own home. The streets in this part of the city are filled with Orientals. Their diminutive figures, oblique set eyes, braided hair, pleasant faces, long black frocks with loose sleeves, and flat, conical crowned hats, attract the curious eye.

In the cellars and on the sidewalks are markets in which dried fish and frogs, strange vegetables, unknowable and indescribable articles of diet are sold. At four p. m. a bell rings and people hurry through the streets to the restaurants. Among them are mild-faced women with babies in their arms; cunning little children in clumsy dresses; little boys with bangles on their ankles. We see them eating unfamiliar dishes, tossing the food into their mouths with chop-sticks. We go into the stores, are fascinated by the strange wares, and make innumerable purchases. The merchant gives preference to some fabrics over others, saying: "This not so best; this more best color, if washee, he no break up." We watch with interest the figuring of the bill upon a wooden frame where wires are stretched, strung with balls of different colors. These fly back and forth under the skilful fingers of the accountant, and almost instantly the sum total is announced.

The manners of the Chinaman are pleasant, their speech quaint, their wares are curious; yet upon many sallow and drawn faces can be seen the shrivelling brand of the opium habit. For the benefit of any who wish to visit the stores I append a few names of the principal business firms, as we noted them during our walk in Chinatown: Wo Sang, Quong Din Kee, Wing On Wah, Yung Lung, Hang Fer Low, Tuck Hop, and, strangest of all, Yan Kee Fun.

The government of China is patriarchal; the religion is mainly ancestor worship. We went into a Joss House or temple, where the few sacred rites are practiced. We entered freely, for the doors always stand open. No fee is required, no janitor is in attendance. On the first floor were arrangements evidently for funeral services. Above was a room decorated with gilt and colored screens, rich embroideries, lamps and bronzes, banners and artificial flowers. An immense amount of wealth had been expended in the decoration of this apartment.

Before a kind of altar in the middle of the room was a covered shelf or table, where round sieves or riddles had been placed, in the perforations of which stood lighted incense sticks. These burned slowly and filled the temple with a pleasant fragrance. The Chinese believe that the spirits of the dead still crave things connected with their former lives, but being of an ethereal nature can receive them only in a sublimated form; all offerings are therefore burned. Behind the altar was a dark recess in which the image of a man was sitting on a throne. His robes were gorgeous, his complexion very dark. We were told that this effigy represented a famous Chinese warrior, brother of one of the early emperors. I think this must have been the famous Tartar Buddha, Sakya Sinha, Lion of the Moon, although the name as given was not identical. There were only ten chairs in this place of worship, five on each side of the altar.

The tea houses or restaurants, are also interesting objects. The fronts of these airy buildings are gay with balconies, verandas, lanterns and streamers—all painted in bright colors, vermillion and green, with a profusion of gilt.

The Chinese embassy arrived during our stay in San Francisco, and were guests at the Palace. The high dignitaries were seldom seen, as they did not condescend to patronize the dining room, but had their meals brought from the Chinese quarters in covered trays.

The western coast is at present suffering from a violent attack of Chinaphobia, a phase, no doubt, of the moral and mental unsettlement that exists all over the world; the same conditions that produce riots, strikes, boycotts and other irrational outbreaks. It is difficult for an unprejudiced observer to discover any cause for antipathy to the Chinese. The universal testimony is that they are patient, diligent, honest; they do their work thoroughly and for small wages. Their faults and vices are common to all crowded populations, and are as patent and abhorrent among white men in London, Paris and New York, as among Chinamen in San Francisco.

The morning after our return from Monterey was lowery; gray, watery clouds streaked the sky; the weather, evidently brooding over some unspoken grievance, to follow the fashion, contemplated a boycott. A faint, luminous break in the clouds gave us courage, and we hastened out to do our shopping. Irresistibly we were drawn toward Chinatown, but soon discovered by antagonistic currents and unfamiliar surroundings, that we had lost our way. We hailed a gigantic policeman, who, in answer to our questions, admitted that we were "in about the worst part of the city," kindly piloted us to the end of his beat, and gave us directions for our further walk.

We entered into the Chinese stores, emptied our purses into the money drawer and took from shelf and counter strange and curious wares.

The threatened rain now began to fall in torrents; a close carriage was procured, our numerous bundles were placed therein, ourselves squeezed in after them and we returned to the hotel. The pouring rain continued and the day closed with a violent storm.

April 10th we woke to find the storm still implacable. A sourer, more sullen, vixenish day I have never seen. The head of the weather, from our windows, appeared utterly dishevelled; the vapors, like unkempt locks, were blown and twisted in every direction; the face of the sky was dark and scowling. Tears, not of grief but rage, fell from its bleared eyes; floods of water were poured from its dripping buckets, drenching the buildings and making rivers of the streets. "How the sleet whipped the panes!"

An ark and an Ararat seemed necessary to rescue the people. Make no more boast of your perfect climate, Mistress California. A gloomier, fouler day upon New England never dawned.

At noon the clouds "stinted," to use a Shakespearism. We took advantage of the propitious moment to call upon friends who had bestowed many kind attentions, but before we returned the rain again set in, poured all the evening and most of the night.

Sunday morning the sun was shining, but a vapory horizon gave token of continued unsettlement of the weather. However, we went to church and heard a sermon upon the unusual and obscure text, "And it repented the Lord that He had made man on the earth, and it grieved Him to the heart." The explanation was unsatisfactory, the argument weak, not even specious. It was a daring attempt to reconcile that which, from the preacher's standpoint, was irreconcilable, while one ray from another direction would have resolved every difficulty.

A number of friends call in the evening to bid us farewell, for the morrow is to witness our departure. That which has been rain on the coast has been snow on the mountains; it is reported four feet deep in the Sierra Nevadas.

Chapter Twelve.

THE RETURN.

PLAINS OF SACRAMENTO—ATMOSPHERIC PHENOMENA—PASSAGE OF THE SIERRA NEVADAS—UNDER THE SNOW-SHEDS—VISIONS OF THE NIGHT—THE GREAT AMERICAN DESERT.

WE left the station at Oakland, April 12th, our faces for the first time turned homeward. The route lay across the plains of Sacramento to the city of that name, now the capital of California. These plains, one hundred miles in length, are exceedingly fertile, but being only fifty feet above the sea level at the highest point, are subject to malarial diseases. The flats were, at the time of our passing them, almost covered with water from the heavy rains. The city is only fifteen feet above the low water mark of the river that runs through it, but the principal streets have been raised, and the banks of the stream protected by levees. A slight volcanic subsidence would make this plain once more an inland sea.

As we left Sacramento, about eight o'clock, we observed a remarkable appearance in the eastern heavens. High up in the clear sky were the great planets Mars, Jupiter and Saturn, and although invisible, we knew that in this same region distant Neptune held his course. Beneath this constellation of planets, near the earth, hung a great cloud in the shape of a roll. We had no means of calculating its size accurately, but it seemed thirty or forty degrees in length and half that number in circumference. The bright moon made the upper portion white as a thunder head, the lower part was of inky blackness, and the earth beneath was cast into a Tartarean shadow. Streaks of black vapor went up to the apex of the cloud, which seemed to be lowering upon the plain. This strange apparition reminded us of descriptions of on-coming earthquakes and cyclones; we wondered if the extraordinary nimbus would overtake and demolish our train; but the swift engine bore us away and the cloud was seen no more.

As I was copying the rough sketch of this cloud a day or two afterward, one of our party read from the Salt Lake Tribune, just brought into the car, an account of the terrible cyclones which struck St. Cloud, Sauk Rapids and other places in Minnesota, and passed over some portions of Illinois, on the morning of the 14th. Was the phenomenon we saw in the eastern sky, twenty hours previously, the nucleus of electrical forces then gathering for such an awful onset?

Shortly after eight o'clock we began the ascent of the Sierre Nevadas. The snow-fall is so deep in the mountains the railroad company have been obliged to build snow-sheds thirty-six miles in length to protect the track. The scenery is said to be very fine; travelers do not see it however, as trains make the trip both ways in the night. Wise management, for no one in his sober senses would dare the perilous feat with his eyes open. Here "ignorance (of one's surroundings) is bliss."

The low rates, and perhaps some vague instinct we may not fathom, has drawn an army of tourists to the Pacific coast this season. The railroad officials find it almost impossible to handle the immense traffic; fifteen private cars stood upon the track at Oakland, the railroad station of San Francisco, at the time we left.

Twenty-three passenger cars went out on our train. These were divided into three sections, with two powerful engines, a pusher and a puller, for each; such an equipment betokened the tremendous labor required. To reach the town of Reno the ponderous machines must force their way up mountain steeps and along sheer precipices till they attain an elevation of nearly seven thousand feet; defying the law of gravitation, battling with wind, snow and midnight shadows, and dragging their burden of loaded cars. As there was nothing to be seen we retired early, and a sense of unusual danger weighed down our spirits as we fell into uneasy dreams.

The night waned; we were conscious that the motion of the train gradually became slower; the cough of the toiling engines was hoarse and intermittent; the sounds peculiar to railroad travel seemed exaggerated and hollow. For hours we had been climbing; where are we now? Misty vagaries float through the brain. Half asleep we murmur a modification of an old Mother Goose refrain:

> "The roof of your wonderful car, sir,
> Has gone up so wonderful high,
> That as the great train rumbles forward,
> It rattles against the sky."

The engines slowed, slowed, then stopped; the noises ceased—we seemed to be sealed up in a cistern! Presently the silence was broken, there was a great commotion among the engines, trumpeting, bellowing, signaling; their voices roared, rolled, reverberated—"One, two, three!" they shrieked. Back came a hollow answer, "One, two, three!"

Again they thundered, "One, two, three!" and now a more distant echo, "One, two, three!"

It was the signal Go!!

Away went section Number One with its rattling train; our section, Number Two, dashed after, followed closely by Number Three, as in a race for life. Down, down they went with reckless speed, the motion each instant increasing; swifter, swifter, as if all the goblins of the mountains were in pursuit of the flying trains.

In vain we strove to dull our sense of danger, to close our ears to the inexplicable sounds, to compel the oblivion of slumber. Our weird and unnatural surroundings mingle with half-waking dreams. We are the solitary Manu of Eastern story, and Vishnu the Preserver, in form of a fish, is dragging us through the waters of the Deluge. The sides of the friendly monster graze a mountain, we are scrambling ashore, when a change comes over the spirit of our dream. The great Roc of Sinbad the Sailor flaps its wings above us; we are seized in its talons and borne aloft through the sky. Just as we are about to fall into the Valley of Diamonds it is changed into the Mediteranean Sea, and lo! we are talking with Jonah in the cabin of his safe but extraordinary craft, which is tearing through the waves at a fearful rate, chased by a Phœnecian whaler. A terrible storm is raging, thunder rumbles overhead, flashes of lightning dazzle our eyes.

We wake with a start to find our car rushing through the last of the snow-sheds; the thunder was the reverberation of the train against the wooden roofs; the lightnings were flashes of sunlight and snow through the infrequent windows. Day had come; the pass of the Sierra Nevada was accomplished; we were at the town of Reno. We rose with aching heads, buzzing ears and all the disagreeable symptoms attendant upon such flights into the clouds, but thankful that another range of mountains walling us from our beloved home had been scaled in safety.

From Wadsworth, Nevada, to Corrienne, Utah, is seven hundred miles; of this only sixty miles is set in the guide books as the Great American Desert, but to the eye of the traveler it extends the entire distance. A more dismal, melancholy scene can scarcely be imagined. One writer in describing it says: "The earth, alkaline and powdered, is whirled up by the least wind into blinding clouds of dust; rivers disappear in it, no kind of vegetation will live save the pallid sage brush. The only animals are lizards and the jack rabbit. The land seems to have been desolated by fire; the blight that oppresses it is indescribable. The serrated mountains that break the level are devoid of vegetation from foot to crest, and are of a dull leaden gray or brown. Sahara itself cannot surpass this desert in woe-begone infertility."

Words do not convey an adequate idea of the gloom of these plains, stretching away in every direction to a wall of frowning mountains that bar out the sky and hem the desert in. At the present time many ranges are covered with snow and display an unusual variety of color effect. The loftiest peaks tower above the vapors and the unclouded sun renders their tops more dazzling than any thunder-head; they are mountains of light. Others, in the shadow of storm clouds, are colorless or of a chilly gray, pale as the ghosts of hills. Sometimes they are heaped in toppling piles against the sky, and again in regular thick set sierra, like the white teeth of a monster shark.

But whether snow-capped or bald, piercing the clouds or lying scattered upon the plain, glittering in noonday sun, purpling in twilight, or rising black under the faint rays of the moon, they are ever present, pursuing the traveler like a waking nightmare, an expected surprise, a familiar wonder; beautiful but terrible in the majesty of desolation.

Chapter Thirteen.

SALT LAKE CITY AND THE MORMONS.

THE CURSE OF POLYGAMY — PUBLIC BUILDINGS — THE ENDOWMENT HOUSE — THE IMPRECATION — BRIGHAM'S FAVORITE — THE WAGES OF SIN.

"Every man shall receive according to the deeds done in the body."

APRIL 14th our way tracked the Great Salt Lake, the Dead Sea of the American continent. It lies among the Wasatch Mountains, is seventy miles long and thirty wide, but very shallow — in some places only two or three feet deep. Although it is four thousand two hundred feet above the ocean, the water is so impregnated with salt a man will float upon the surface if his arms are extended; taken into the mouth it causes strangulation, and a drop in the eye burns like fire. No fish can live in these noxious waters, and though several rivers empty into the basin there is no outlet. About eight miles south of this anomalous inland sea, upon a level amphitheatre formed by the Wasatch Mountains, the notorious apostle of Mormonism founded his city.

Soon after our arrival we took a carriage and drove to the heights above, where a fine view is obtained. The dark blue mountains were covered with new fallen snow, affording a contrast of exceeding beauty. A sluggish river, called the Jordan, winds through the fertile plain like a loose ribbon. The streets of the city, one hundred and twenty-eight feet wide, are regularly laid out according to the points of the compass. They are well-shaded and furnished on each side with open conduits of water that freshen the air and carry off all impurity— *no, not quite all!* Some of the modern dwellings are fine; particularly noticeable is that of George Q. Cannon, representative to Congress, a Mormon, a polygamist, and at present a fugitive from justice. He has broken his bail, forty-five thousand dollars, which the deluded disciples must pay. The older houses are of wood, low, mean, and in construction suggestive. They almost always have two front doors, we saw some with three.

There are thirty thousand inhabitants in the city, and in each of the twenty-three wards is a meeting house and Zion's Co-operative Mercantile Association, over the doors of which are placed the All-Seeing Eye and the legend, "Holiness to the Lord." As we looked upon these blasphemous appeals to a God of purity and love, our thoughts reverted almost with complaisancy to the El Paso sign board, "Jesus C. Dobie, Liquor Dealer." The aspect of the people we saw at this time and afterward, as we walked the streets, was so forbidding that we could but exclaim with an English poet, "Oh, God, what base, ignoble faces!" Those of the old men are what we call hard; that is, selfish, sensual, cunning, cruel; the younger men are bold, impudent, boisterous—first-class rowdies. The women — but I spare them!

Almost the entire population are Mormons, between whom and the Christians irreconcilable enmity exists. The latter say that Eastern people have no conception of the horrors of the system. Young girls run away from home and take up the ignominious life of a mining camp rather than be sealed to a Mormon. The brutality of Mormon husbands is most revolting. A man told us he heard Brigham Young say from the pulpit, "Turn your wives out into the field, compel them to gather the crops: if you can't get enough without, take squaws."

A young Englishman became a convert under the teachings of a Mormon missionary and brought his young wife to Utah. One of the elders coveted this woman. He sent the husband away on some distant expedition, and during his absence visited the wife and told her his desire. She said: "But I am already married. I love my husband and I cannot be your wife." "Oh, I can get a divorce easily," said he. But the woman would not listen. Soon after she disappeared, and the wicked elder, under dreadful threats, compelled the neighbors to declare when the husband returned, that his wife had run away with another man.

The elder was a confirmed drunkard, and during a debauch he exposed the fact that he had murdered the woman, thrown her into a well and filled it with earth and stones. No one dared investigate till the elder died; then the well was opened and the mangled body was found. A lady who had seen the husband told me he was from the time of his misfortune a silent, melancholy, broken-hearted man, but he had never dared to complain. There is no hope of justice in Mormon courts. The most flagrant outrages and fiendish crimes are not only connived at, but actually planned by the highest officials, who, if their own necks are imperilled by the possibility of exposure, will ruthlessly sacrifice their miserable agents.

But enough—I will not pain my readers by transcribing the chapter of horrors related by credible witnesses; yet there is one true story in which the pathetic and ludicrous meet in a manner to rival any fiction of Charles Dickens, which I am tempted to repeat.

Miss Sybil Carter, who was sent out by the New West Educational Commission relates the following experience:

"Once a curious thing happened. A very ugly looking man came to the school house to do some repairing. After it was completed I began to wish he would go, but as he lingered I asked: "Is there anything more to be done?"

"Oh," said he, "I shouldn't wonder if you all in the States hated us!"

There was something bitter and strange in his manner.

I said, "Well, the old times are gone by, and they will not come back any more."

"But they would," he said, "if Brigham wasn't dead. I'm glad Brigham's dead!"

"So am I," said I, "if that is the way it is — but let the old times go, and don't think of them. Think of something better."

But he replied, "Brigham made us do some awful things, and we would have had our own throats cut if we had refused. Once Brigham called out fifty-four men — four came from Lehi. There is one there now who was among them. They had three hundred Indians who were to act as spies on the Mormons." Then he told me the whole details of one of the cruel Mormon excursions. Among other things he said the victims were suffering with thirst and sent a little girl with a pitcher to a spring to get some water. The child started off but had not run a dozen yards when she fell pierced with twenty bullets. He said he had never since closed his eyes without seeing the little girl with the white dress and long yellow curls. I was so impressed with the evident sorrow and remorse of the man for these things in which he had, though unwillingly, partaken, that I asked him if he did not want to get right down on his knees and ask God to forgive him. Then I knelt and prayed with all my heart. Before I could think, he knelt down too, and made this prayer. It was so short I shall never forget it:

"Lord God Almighty, I ain't much used to talking with ye, but I want you to hear every word this young woman has said, and I'll never do it again — you bet!"

The principal public buildings in Salt Lake City belong to this detestable sect, and are in a walled enclosure called Temple Block. The principal one is the Tabernacle, an immense circular building with a dome for a roof, an awkward but commodious edifice, capable of seating ten thousand persons. At the time of our visit the great ceiling was profusely decorated with faded evergreen wreaths. "These," I said to the guide, "are presumably Christmas wreaths." "No," he replied, "they were put there for a Sunday school festival in 1875. It was found they did not *deteriorate the costic properties*, so they are left." Literary accuracy is evidently not among the Mormon accomplishments.

The church proper, a small, ornate building, is used in severely cold weather, being more easily heated than the Tabernacle. While viewing the frescoes of this church, which are in singular taste, being representations of other Mormon temples depicted on the ceiling, our attention was drawn to a colossal painting over the gallery.

"This," said the guide, "is Maroni telling the young man where to find the golden tablets—the Mormon Bible."

"Who is Maroni?" I innocently asked.

"He is one of the three. There was Maroni, Lehi and Mormon."

"Then Mormon was a man."

"Yes. The three led the people of this country as Moses led the children of Israel out of the wilderness. There were people in this country."

"Ah," said I. "Who is the young man?"

"Why, that is Joseph Smith."

"When did this happen?"

"In 1830, near Palmyra, New York."

"Where are the tablets now?"

"Why, they are—they are—most of them withdrawn up into the—into the divine."

This all as soberly as a child repeating a fable, but it is not possible the man believed what he was saying.

Another building in this enclosure is called the Endowment House. Why endowment I cannot imagine, for everything worth living for in a woman's life is here taken away. In this den the secret rites of Mormonism are practiced, or rather perpetrated, and marriages are enforced on unwilling victims. Here poor helpless women have been endowed with their half, or tenth, or twentieth part of a husband, as the case might be, by the hand of the devil in the likeness of Brigham Young.

The formula of the horrible threat and imprecation used at the Endowment House is given as follows by one who escaped from bondage:

THE THREAT.

"If you repeat anything relating to the ceremonies through which you have already passed, your throat will be cut from ear to ear."

THE SELF-IMPRECATION.

"If ever I reveal the secrets of this house, may my tongue be torn out by the roots, my heart and bowels cut out while I am yet alive; and if I escape in this world, may all these penalties overtake me in the morning of the Resurrection."

Oh, the heartaches, the bitterness, the smothered agony, the cries unavailing these walls have witnessed; the brutish sensuality, the fiendish cruelty which have in this accursed building leered or glared from under a religious cloak!

But the most imposing structure in this citadel of Satan is the Temple—a magnificent white granite edifice, commenced in 1853 and still in process of construction. The cost will be ten millions of dollars, wrung from the toil of fanatical men and women. The walls are mostly finished, the towers and roofs are to be added and the interior constructed. On the front and rear walls are carved medallions, representing two clasped hands. If this means Mormon marriage, the fundamental idea of this infernal institution, why not place a man's hand on one side and a dozen or more slender wrists on the other, not joined in a clasp, but a clutch.

Above the hands on the upper stories are other medallions on which are carved, so the guide told us, THE ALL-SEEING EYE, and over this device the legend, HOLINESS TO THE LORD. The eye on the rear wall is apparently overlooking the Endowment House. Audacious blasphemy! Why does not the indignant stone transform itself into a Medusa Head and petrify the blasphemers? The Temple is not designed as a place of worship, but for the performance of the secret rites. I looked down into the subterranean vaults walled in with stone, I shuddered and hastened away from the unholy precincts.

On the opposite street, in another walled enclosure, stands the Tithing House, to which infatuated disciples from all parts of the territory bring tithes of all they possess, a practice which keeps the lower classes poverty stricken. Here we saw men of degraded aspect, driving wagons loaded with various farm products into the large barn-yards. In the house was a meat market and many other untidy apartments. Beyond the Tithing House, but in the same enclosure, are the Lion House and the Bee House, so called from images of these objects placed upon the apex of the roofs. The use of these last named buildings I did not learn.

Opposite these nondescripts, on the other side of the main street, is a large, elegant and pretentious dwelling-house, called Amelia's Palace, built by Brigham Young for his favorite wife. Why his favorite? With what, I hope, was a pardonable curiosity, I strove to learn the secret of Amelia's power over this Yankee Mahommetan. For some time I was unsuccessful, but at length I met an honest man, a Gentile, who had been a resident of Salt Lake City for many years, and the following conversation, ensued:

"How many children survive Brigham, and are they sons or daughters?"

"He left fifty children, mostly daughters."

"What of their character?"

"The sons are most of them drunkards, and some of the daughters lead disreputable lives. Each one had forty thousand dollars, but the money is being squandered rapidly. The Mormons are very intemperate. I never saw men who could equal them in drinking."

"Excuse me, but I wish to learn the secret of Amelia's power. Was she more beautiful than the other seventeen, or, as some say, sixty-eight (a few more or less makes no difference now), who shared the attenuated affection of her lord?"

"No, she was well enough in looks, but not handsome."

"Was she younger, more accomplished, intelligent, graceful?"

"None of these!"

"What then was the secret of her power?" I urged, for the investigation was becoming very interesting.

After a moment of hesitation he replied directly to the point: "A strong will and a terrible temper. If things didn't go to suit Amelia she raised a storm, actually broke up furniture and smashed things."

I did not answer, but mentally made a note of this fact as a valuable lesson to wives—similarly situated.

When Brigham died, his successor, John Taylor, took possession of the palace and turned Amelia into very humble quarters.

All the property in these walled enclosures, and a great deal beside, to the amount of ten millions it is said, belonged to Brigham. He does not own it now—he does not even care for it—he has gone a long journey to settle an account that had been running eighty-four years. That settlement has left him a beggar with a heavy debt on his hands; willing or unwilling, he must pay it. He was a lord once, an inexorable tyrant, cruel, unrelenting; men obeyed him trembling—or had their throats cut. Now he is a slave chained to a mountain of sin, a mountain of his own raising, chains of his own forging. He does not struggle, he knows it would be in vain, he cannot forget, he cannot close his eyes to the dreadful visions that float before him — the Danites at their hellish work, the fainting wives and mothers as they discover the dead bodies upon the doorsteps; the ruthless murder of his helpless agents when their testimony might implicate himself.

"Dead men tell no tales," said Brigham. Now he groans as he perceives his error. He shudders as the phantom host of Mountain Meadow stalk by and mock him, but he falls in abject terror before the spectre of a child, a little girl whose golden locks and snow white robes are dabbled with blood, who points her ghostly finger and shrieks, "I tell thee thou comest not hence, until thou has paid the uttermost farthing."

This apostle of darkness is sometimes called sagacious. A sagacious man calculates remote consequences, Brigham did not — or still worse, he defied them. Vain and miserable defiance, "an hour cometh that will requite all."

I saw the spot where his body, the instrument of his evil will, moulders in the earth and defiles the grass that grows above it. God grant that I may never see the prison where his disembodied spirit "awaits in chains and darkness the judgment of the last great day."

Chapter Fourteen.

HOMEWARD BOUND.

WEBER CANYON—ECHO CANYON—CHEYENE—OMAHA
—AU REVOIR—ALL HAIL VERMONT.

AT four o'clock p. m. we left Salt Lake City and ran down to Ogden, thirty-seven miles, to spend the night—glad to escape from a moral atmosphere so tainted; but full of pity for the Gentiles still compelled by circumstances to breathe the polluted air.

Friday morning, April 16th, we resumed our journey. Twenty miles east of Ogden we entered the Weber Canyon. The approach to this remarkable gorge is through a bold, craggy pass, called the Devil's Gate. It is a place of awful gloom; overhanging rocks darken the air and make a mid-day twilight that chills the body and weighs down the spirit. A muddy stream roars through the defile and a blast of wind rushes by like a troop of spectres.

The stony peaks, eroded and eaten by the tooth of time, have assumed strange, fantastic shapes; they loom up like chimneys, towers, buttresses, fortifications pierced with holes as for cannon, castles, hieroglyphs, grotesque forms like Aztec gods. In one instance a group of rocks forcibly reminded us of

Vedder's illustration of the verse in the Rubyat that reads thus:

> "They say the lion and the lizard keep
> Their court where Jamshed gloried and drank deep,
> And Baram, that great hunter, the wild ass
> Stamps o'er his head, but cannot break his sleep."

Indeed the whole scene is suggestive of that grand and gloomy poem.

There must have been giants of old, legions of them, to have upreared such stupendous monuments. In this canyon there is an extraordinary and anomalous formation, known as the Devil's Slide. Two walls of rock, perpendicular and parallel as the paling of a fence, run up the frightful steep of a frowning cliff, making an even, narrow lane utterly unlike anything else in the vicinity. But if the evil one made his descent from the mountain in this dangerous slide, the fall was not fatal. He recovered, went through his gate to the west and settled in Salt Lake City, where he now carries on a thriving business.

A few miles further on is Echo Canyon, less striking than the other, but unique from the prevalence of a red color in the rocks that contrasts beautifully with carpets of gray-green sage brush by which the shelves are covered and softened.

Nature seems to have selected these wild mountains for her waste places—here the demiurges have piled up or scattered the debris of creation.

Saturday morning, April 17th, we awoke to find ourselves at Laramie, in the Black Hills, a spur of the Rockies. The earth was covered with snow for one hundred miles. We continued to ascend until we reached Sherman, the height of land eight thousand two hundred and thirty-five feet, one hundred and thirty-three feet higher than Marquez, the highest point on the Mexican Central. Think of a train of cars up in the sky at this awful altitude; nearly twice as high as the top of Mansfield Mountain. In this lofty city a plain but massive monument has been erected to the memory of Oakes Ames, the first president of the Union Pacific road.

At eleven a. m. we passed Cheyene, seven thousand inhabitants, said to be the richest city of its size in the United States. Sunday we spent at Omaha, Nebraska, a thriving city of sixty thousand souls. Coming out of church we met our old neighbor, Charles Samson, his mother, wife and sister. They are well and happy, but like scores of other New Englanders we have seen, they sigh for the salubrious air and social life of the East.

We have met a large number of graduates from the Central Vermont railroad, and are happy to know how highly successful and universally respected they have become in their new positions. And the unmistakable joy that beamed in every face upon our unexpected meetings was a gratifying indication of the love they still cherish for their Alma Mater.

Sunday night and Monday we passed through the highly cultivated lands of Iowa and Illinois, reaching Chicago at half-past two p. m., March 19th.

And now, dear reader, I will trouble you no longer. By the magic power of the pen we have journeyed together more than eleven thousand miles and through the kindness of an overruling Providence no trouble has come nigh us. We have scaled mountain heights where the snow forever rests, we have sailed on tropic seas and groped in dungeons dank, we have hung breathless on slender wires over yawning chasms, and crossed dreary deserts, have inhaled the soft airs of Eden and stifled in the miasma of Mormonism. I have gathered for your acceptance flowers of fancy from perrenial gardens and fruits of thought from citrus groves.

But now we have reached the beaten paths of travel, where every scene is familiar and the rude footsteps of a hurrying throng crush out the tender buds of sentiment, and rather than offer platitudes and commonplaces I will bid you a kind FAREWELL.

"EAST OR WEST—HOME IS BEST."

"Here where there's ice and snow,
Here where the cold winds blow,
Our hearts and footsteps go,
   To thee—Vermont!
Thou art our native state,
No place can be thy mate,
Thou hast no duplicate,
   Beloved Vermont.

"In every passing breeze,
In all the grassy leas,
The true Vermonter sees
   His dear old home.
In lands far, far away,
He longeth for the day
When joyful he can say,
   I'm bound for home."

www.ingramcontent.com/pod-product-compliance
Lightning Source LLC
Chambersburg PA
CBHW022141160426
43197CB00009B/1382